Strategic
Listening
F O R
School
Leaders

Strategic Listening

F O R

School Leaders

JEANNINE S. TATE   DENNIS R. DUNKLEE

FOREWORD BY ROLAND S. BARTH

CORWIN PRESS
A SAGE Publications Company
Thousand Oaks, California

For information:

Corwin Press
A Sage Publications Company
2455 Teller Road
Thousand Oaks, California 91320
www.corwinpress.com

Sage Publications Ltd.
1 Oliver's Yard
55 City Road
London EC1Y 1SP
United Kingdom

Sage Publications India Pvt. Ltd.
B-42, Panchsheel Enclave
Post Box 4109
New Delhi 110 017 India

Printed in the United States of America

Library of Congress Cataloging-in-Publication Data

Tate, Jeannine S.
Strategic listening for school leaders/Jeannine S. Tate and Dennis R. Dunklee.
        p. cm.
Includes bibliographical references and index.
ISBN 1-4129-1330-6 (cloth) — ISBN 1-4129-1331-4 (pbk.)
    1. School personnel management. 2. Communication in education. 3. Listening.
I. Dunklee, Dennis R. II. Title.
LB2831.5.T38 2005
371.2′01—dc22   2004028780

This book is printed on acid-free paper.

05   06   07   08   09   10   9   8   7   6   5   4   3   2   1

Acquisitions Editor:	Elizabeth Brenkus
Editorial Assistant:	Candice L. Ling
Production Editor:	Beth A. Bernstein
Copy Editor:	Stacey Shimizu
Typesetter:	C&M Digitals (P) Ltd.
Proofreader:	Liann Lech
Indexer:	Naomi Linzer
Cover Designer:	Rose Storey

Contents

Foreword

"There's more to listening than meets the ear!" That's the refreshing message of this welcome little volume. People tend to choose a career in teaching because they like to talk. It's been estimated that about 85% of the time, teachers rely on didactic, large- and small-group instruction. Those teachers who become administrators like to talk even more. And all educators like to be listened to every bit as much as they like to talk.

Unfortunately, talk is as limited a form of teaching as it is of leading. Brain research, for instance, now tells us that students can benefit from only as many minutes of teacher talk as their age in years. That's 10 minutes for fourth graders, 15 minutes for ninth graders.

And, as we all know, adults have their limits, too! How long can the faculty listen to the principal progress through the never-ending checklist at the biweekly staff meeting before they begin to grade their homework papers? How long can the superintendent's administrative team of principals benefit from an explication of the new mandates before they tune out? Not as long as most have to.

So, how is one to teach or lead if one doesn't talk? The many helpful, often revolutionary messages offered in these pages provide a powerful answer: We can learn to listen! Listen strategically.

It's not clear to me why strategic listening has been so overlooked as an active art form in the school leader's repertoire. Fortunately, with the thoughtful ideas offered here, it need be neglected no longer.

Our ververbal profession desperately needs to recognize that there are as many ways to listen as there are different purposes for listening. Here, we learn about listening to understand, to find shared meaning, and to understand assumptions; discriminative listening; comprehensive listening; therapeutic listening; critical listening; and listening for conflict management and resolution. These thoughtful, intentional listening skills will sensitize all of us educators to the power of listening and will help us learn to lead through listening.

For school leaders, this tool kit is a "two-fer." By learning to listen strategically, one can bring out the best of which others are capable more of the time. And that, after all, is what leadership is all about. But the benefits do not stop there. The principal who learns how to listen to teachers models a behavior that teachers will soon exhibit in turn in their interactions with students—a most welcome ripple effect.

The bottom line is that educators can effectively lead students and adults as much through strategic listening as by prolonged speaking. So, I commend to you the rich description and analysis of the art of listening that you are about to experience. A powerful way to build a professional learning community is to build a community of strategic listeners!

—*Roland S. Barth*

Preface

I speak because I know my needs,
I speak with hesitation because I know not yours.
My words come from my life's experiences,
Your understanding comes from yours.
Because of this,
What I say, and what you hear,
May not be the same.
So if you will listen carefully,
Not only with your ears,
But with your eyes and with your heart,
Maybe somehow we can communicate.

—*Herbert G. Lingren*

Not too long ago, an effective school leader hired teachers, monitored the curriculum, ordered books, upheld discipline, and maintained the building and grounds. In recent years, with the No Child Left Behind Act, standards-based curricula, and an ever-increasing push for accountability by an ever more demanding public, school leaders have faced unprecedented challenges. The ability to maintain leadership in the education enterprise hinges on the leader's ability to communicate effectively with multiple constituencies. Listening is an essential function of the communication process.

The Greek philosopher Epictetus noted that "nature gave us one tongue and two ears so we could hear twice as much as we speak." We believe he was speaking directly to us—as opposed to politicians—when he made this declaration. Ernest Hemingway wrote, "I like to listen. I have

SOURCE: The poem by Herbert G. Lingren is used with permission of Cooperative Extension Division, University of Nebraska Institute of Agriculture and Technology.

learned a great deal from listening carefully. Most people never listen." We learned, very early in our respective careers in education, that you really can't listen when you're talking.

In a linear environment, effective communication is characterized by a leader's ability to give clear directions and prepare cogent reports. For many reasons, we, along with most of the readers of this book, choose to teach, manage, and lead in the nonlinear environment of the school culture—an environment in which we are required, often minute by minute, to respond appropriately to highly diverse constituencies. Our first challenge is to be able to listen effectively to what those constituents expect. We find it calming, in the often declamatory atmosphere of our nonlinear profession, to remember this old Scottish verse: "His thoughts were slow, his words were few, and never formed to glisten. But he was a joy for all his clan, for you should have heard him listen!"

This book focuses on an effective style of listening that we call *strategic listening*. We present the basic theories that underlie strategic listening, succinct examples of strategic listening in practice (how-tos), and persuasive arguments regarding the positive impact and advantages strategic listening affords school leaders. We feel strongly about strategic listening, and we use our successes over a combined 70 years of practice in the education profession as a background to demonstrate that strategic listening is a vital interpersonal skill for principals and other education professionals who lead their organizations successfully. We use strategic listening as an integral part of our communication methodology to enhance our ability to understand others' strengths and weaknesses, and most important, what motivates them.

We believe that strategic listening has provided us with the opportunity to achieve win-win solutions to problems; to communicate in a way that fosters understanding, affirmation, validation, and appreciation; and to employ the kind of personal interaction that creates an atmosphere of trust, honor, and respect. Strategic listening is a skill that everyone can develop. We hope you find that our approach to developing strategic listening skills helps you advance your overall communication expertise.

ACKNOWLEDGMENTS

I want to thank those people who inspired, guided, and encouraged me: my late father, Bill Seeds, who fiercely believed there is no higher calling than teaching or the ministry; my mother, Joe Ann, who showed me how to listen; Jim, Jackie, and Jeff Tate, the lights of my life; Dennis Dunklee, my teacher, mentor, and coauthor, who believed in me; our editor at The SGD

Writing Center, who tactfully helped me rearrange my words; Rob Clouse and Lizzie Brenkus of Corwin Press, who gave me a chance to share some hard-earned wisdom; and to all the teachers and staff members with whom I've worked who have their own stories we all need to hear.

—*Jeannine S. Tate*

Recognizing that it's customary to dedicate a book to those people in your life that make it a special place to be, and that the usual dedication is directed toward family, I choose to depart from that custom and thank Jeannine Tate for the opportunity to be a part of this book. Teachers, school administrators, and, yes, even seasoned professors take special pleasure in being able to see their former students grow and flourish in their profession—and, in Jeannine's case, their professional as well as their academic lives. I am envious of Jeannine and her lifelong efforts to make teaching and learning better for her students and colleagues. As a mentor, I'm pleased; as a professor, I'm proud; and as a friend, Jeannine has been and continues to be a pleasure to work with.

—*Dennis R. Dunklee*

The authors and Corwin Press gratefully acknowledge the contributions of the following individuals:

Julie Boyd, Principal
Ashburn Elementary School
Ashburn, VA

Robert Calfee, Professor
School of Education
University of California, Riverside
Riverside, CA

Jeffrey Cornejo, Co-Principal
Millikan High School
Long Beach, CA

Mike Drummond, Principal
Cedar Point Elementary School
Bristow, VA

Richard Flynn, Assistant Professor
College of Education
Murray State University
Murray, KY

Linda Leibert, Principal
Benton Middle School
Manassas, VA

Nancy Moga, Principal
Callaghan Elementary School
Covington, VA

Terry Orr, Associate Professor
Teachers College
Columbia University
New York, NY

Michael Purdy, Coordinator, Professor
Communications Program
College of Arts and Sciences
Governors State University
University Park, IL

Craig Richards, Professor
Teachers College
Columbia University
New York, NY

Carol Robinson, Principal
Jackson Middle School
Falls Church, VA

Judy Smith, Principal, Coach/Mentor
Southern California Comprehensive Assistance Center
Los Angeles County Office of Education
Seal Beach, CA

Katherine Taber, Principal
Jefferson Elementary School
Norman, OK

Paulette Tetteris-Woosley, Assistant Principal
Hasty Elementary School
Thomasville, NC

Megan Tschannen-Moran, Assistant Professor
School of Education
College of William & Mary
Williamsburg, VA

About the Authors

Jeannine S. Tate is principal of Clermont Elementary School in Alexandria, Virginia. During her 25 years in public schools, she has served as both a teacher and a school counselor at the elementary and middle school levels and as an elementary school assistant principal and principal, and she has held various central office positions. She is active in the National Association of Elementary School Principals, the International Listening Association, and Phi Delta Kappa. She has presented papers internationally and conducts inservice presentations to local, state, and national audiences.

Dr. Tate received her PhD in education leadership from George Mason University. Her area of research was in leadership and communication, and her dissertation focused on school leaders and the value of listening. She holds a BS in elementary education from Oklahoma State University and a MEd in guidance and counseling from the University of Oklahoma.

Dennis R. Dunklee is Associate Professor in the Education Leadership Department in the Graduate School of Education at George Mason University. During his 25 years in public schools, he has served as a teacher, elementary school principal, junior high and middle school principal, high school principal, and central office administrator. He teaches courses in education law, school administration, and school business management, and he serves as an advisor and chair for master's and doctoral candidates in school leadership and community college leadership.

Dr. Dunklee received his PhD in school administration and foundations from Kansas State University. His major area of research was in the field of education law, and his dissertation was on tort liability for negligence. He holds a MA in elementary and secondary school administration from Washburn University. Because of his expertise and practical experience, Dr. Dunklee is frequently called on to consult in the areas of effective schools, school law, administrator evaluation, instructional supervision, school-community relations, problem solving, and conflict resolution. In addition, he has been involved as a consultant and expert witness in numerous school-related lawsuits nationwide. As a university scholar and researcher, he has published seven textbooks, two monographs, and more than 75 articles on issues in the fields of school law, business management, administrative practice, and leadership theory. He is active in a number of professional organizations; has presented papers at national, regional, state, and local conferences; and is a widely sought-after clinician for inservice workshops.

This is Dr. Dunklee's fourth book for Corwin Press. His other Corwin books are *You Sound Taller on the Telephone: A Practitioner's View of the Principalship* (1999); *If You Want to Lead, Not Just Manage* (2000); and *The Principal's Quick Reference Guide to School Law* (2002).

Part I

Strategic Listening in Theory

1 Understanding the Basics of Strategic Listening

The reward for always listening when you'd rather be talking is wisdom.

—Anonymous

The world is full of sounds, and so is the schoolhouse. Sounds emanate from everywhere and bounce off walls and down corridors. A principal walks through a barrage of sounds and words every working day. Sometimes, there is so much sound that it's hard to listen.

DO YOU HAVE A MINUTE?

Do you remember the last time you walked into your school building after a meeting in the central office that went on longer than you expected? It may have gone something like this.

You shoulder your way through the front door of the school with a briefcase and lunch bag in one hand, an armload of folders and miscellaneous paperwork in the other, and a head full of what you plan to accomplish before the day is over. The rising sounds of students' voices and the clatter of lunch trays spill into the front hall from the open doors of the cafeteria.

If you're an elementary principal, perhaps before taking two steps, you are pulled up short as a parade of first graders marches by on the way to the playground. Two students wave wildly to get your attention, point to their open mouths, and proudly cry, "Look!" You admire the new gaps in their teeth. If you're a secondary principal, perhaps you are met by a group of students who proudly want to share the results of their SATs.

At any level, K–12, you could be met by a teacher who tells you in a tired voice, "Allen's mom called this morning. She wants to have a conference with you." You wonder, "When does Allen's mom *not* want a conference?"

Two steps later, the head custodian approaches with a scowl, "Frank just called in sick and he won't be in to work the night shift. It's too late to get a replacement. If you need me for the program tonight, it'll be over-time." "Right," you think. "It would be nice if I had a budget for overtime."

As you reach the door to the outer office, the counselor sweeps by say-ing, "We need to meet before 2:00. We just got news about Sara's family, and it's bad." You're afraid that you know what the bad news is and you're not sure you want to hear it.

Inside the office, the attendance secretary touches your arm as you greet her and try to keep moving. "Mr. Jones is furious that you told him his daughter can't stay here because they've moved out of our attendance area. He's says he's coming back this afternoon with his cousin, the lawyer." You sigh as you begin mentally to prepare for a stressful commu-nity relations session with Mr. Jones and part of his extended family.

Continuing on to your office, as you look longingly at the door of the restroom, your secretary says, "You might want to look at that stack of phone messages on your desk right away." She pauses significantly. "The one on top is from the superintendent." Hmm. You search through your memory to try to figure out what that call might be about and hope that it's something good.

As you pass her desk, you notice that the chair outside your door is occupied by Tommy Henderson . . . again. Without prompting, your favorite student holds up both hands and says in a voice rife with indig-nity, "I didn't do it." Uh-huh. He's just going to have to sit there and wait this time.

Finally, inside the sanctity of your office, you take a quick breath. One of the special education teachers leans into the room, smiles brightly, and asks, "Do you have a minute?"

Your first thought is, probably, "Can't I put my stuff down first?"

LISTENING TO UNDERSTAND

In *If You Want to Lead, Not Just Manage,* Dunklee (2000) described an effective principal as one who leads a school and the profession forward—always keeping a primary focus on mission, improvement, and distinction. In order to be an effective school leader, you must understand the concerns and interests of your constituents so that you can bring them together to accomplish the goals of the school. This means that you must listen carefully in order to make sense of your day-to-day life at work.

Strategic listening is more complex than the simple act of hearing. Francis L. Lederer (2000), a physician, wrote, "Sound is a series of vibrations moving as waves through air or other gases, liquids, or solids. Detection of these vibrations, or sound waves, is called hearing." Strategic listening is more than hearing sounds; *strategic listening is listening to understand.*

As effective school leaders, you understand the day-to-day experiences of your faculty, staff, students, and parents. You know what they worry about; what motivates them; what frustrates them; and what they think, feel, and need as they go about their work. In order to do this, you listen to the concerns and interests of the people with whom you work. By listening strategically, school leaders—you—gain the ability to understand your constituents' most serious professional and personal concerns (Marlow, 1992).

Quite often we assume that listening is simply a matter of focusing on the speaker. However, effective school leaders must sincerely *want* to listen and must have the patience and willingness to be of assistance to their faculty, staff, students, and parents. You need to listen respectfully and attend to the emotions, needs, and concerns of those who are trying to communicate with you (Purdy, 1997). This, in a nutshell, is the essence of strategic listening.

Let's look at an example. Phil, one of your teachers, sticks his head in the door one afternoon and says, "I need to leave 30 minutes early today." If you simply *hear* him, you might say, "Uh, Phil. You're not giving me much notice." Or you might say, "Sure. Just fill out a leave slip."

However, if you've been listening strategically, observing his body language, and incorporating your previous knowledge of Phil, you know that his wife is having a very difficult pregnancy and has been told by her doctor to stay in bed. You also know that Phil never schedules appointments during the school day and that he hasn't asked to leave the building early in all the years you've worked together.

"Of course you can," you say as you motion him into the office. "What's up?" You see that he's nervous, and you can hear the tension in his voice.

"It's Allison. She just called and sounded upset. She's bleeding a little, and the doctor wants to see her at 3:00."

"Why don't you go now?" you say. "We can cover for you." He looks relieved, says thanks, and hurries away. By listening carefully and strategically to Phil, you were able to be of real help to him and his wife. It is likely that he will remember this specific instance of genuine concern and return the kindness with continued hard work and loyalty.

Listening is a vitally important part of communication. At work, strategic listening is a tool to gather information that has a bearing on both leadership and management decisions. More important, strategic listening is a way of making teachers and others feel that their ideas and beliefs are of value.

In *A Passion for Excellence: The Leadership Difference*, Peters and Austin (1985) described a leadership technique they called *management by walking around* (MBWA). They wrote of the power listening has for managers who move about the workplace in order to be in touch and make connections with workers. Peters and Austin defined being in touch as a "tangible, visceral way of being informed" (p. 8). They received firsthand knowledge regarding the world of their workers and an understanding of their employees' worldviews by engaging in the three major activities of MBWA: listening, teaching, and facilitating. With a focus on listening, leaders develop empathy for others' perspectives (Peters & Austin, 1985).

As a principal, you never know what you'll discover as you roam around the school. Suppose one afternoon you drop by Evelyn's classroom during her planning period. Your sole intention is to drop off a telephone message on the way to check on a group in the library. Evelyn cannot be described as a star teacher in any sense of the word. In fact, earlier in the week, you gave her an excellent book that explains in detail how to implement a specific strategy that she is not incorporating appropriately into her teaching. Working with her can be especially challenging, because she tends to be sarcastic and defensive during your conversations about instruction.

When you open the door to her room, you are stunned to see Evelyn hunched over a table at the side of the room. She is meticulously finishing a handmade chart she adapted from the book you gave her. On the floor is a stack of at least a dozen more multicolored charts that she has been toiling over. Even though copying charts was not what you had in mind when you gave her the book, you know from the look on her face and the evidence all around that she has taken your advice much more seriously than you could ever have imagined. In that instant, you know that Evelyn wants to do things right; she just needed examples of how to do it. You might never have known this had you not dropped by her room.

"Listening" to nonverbal communication is an important part of strategic listening. If you'd heard only her sarcasm, you'd have missed an important chance to lead.

LISTENING FOR SHARED MEANING

There is a saying that, although it has been seriously overused, still sends a powerful message. Depending on the source, the adage goes something like this: "You should not judge a man until you've walked a mile in his shoes." The same is true about listening. You can't truly understand the meaning of what someone says until you take a look at the world through his or her eyes.

Leading organizations is about bringing people together to accomplish specific goals, and much of leading is about recognizing and appreciating different perspectives. It's important to remember that language is a medium that is most effective when used to create meaning and shared understanding rather than simply to share information. Many principals are not aware that there are almost endless things that can affect individuals' perceptions when they talk to one another.

In a given year, you might have brand-new teachers working beside teachers nearing retirement. You'll have single teachers, married teachers, and teachers in alternative relationships. You might have teachers raised in urban settings, rural settings, and suburban settings. It is more and more likely that you may have teachers from a vast array of religious backgrounds as well as those who claim no religious faith at all. We could name dozens of other factors that can affect a person's perspective on life, but the bottom line is this: Trying to understand a person's perspective is an important part of strategic listening.

Meaning is unique and appropriate to the situation and to the people in the situation. Because what is being talked about comes from two or more sets of experiences, you and the other person must offer each other the opportunity to contribute to the development of shared meaning (Shotter, 1993). The more sensitive you are to the fact that everyone filters conversations through his or her own unique set of beliefs and experiences, the closer you are to understanding the needs and motivations of your faculty and staff. That understanding can lead you to the development of shared meaning and a more effective way of accomplishing the goals of your schools.

Listening for shared meaning is hard work. You can probably think of a time when you looked at someone with whom you were speaking and wondered, "Did he understand what I just said?" It's likely that the listener was thinking, "What did she mean by that?" Broomhilda, a popular cartoon character, always has an interesting outlook on the world. Russell Myers, her creator, provided the following conversation between Broomhilda and Nerwin in his March 5, 2004, strip in the *Washington Post*: Nerwin, that funny little character with the propeller beanie, says to Broomhilda, "I'm goin' over to Artie's to play." Broomhilda responds, "Be home by six on the dot, Nerwin." As Nerwin walks away, Broomhilda asks, "Now what did I just tell you?" Nerwin's response is, "Uh . . . have fun, see you later?" Broomhilda looks directly at the reader with a questioning expression on her face and says, "The words sound okay when they come out of my mouth, so what happens to them after that?"

It has been said that "all observers are not led by the same physical evidence to the same picture of the universe" (Schrange, 1989, p. 69). This fact can lead to some interesting mix-ups. For example, envision a cold, dark afternoon in the dead of winter at school when it begins to snow. Soon, it is apparent that the storm is well on the way to becoming a full-fledged blizzard. Being the sensitive and caring principal you are, you send a note to the teachers saying that they may leave as soon as the students are gone.

At dismissal time, you're standing in the parking lot directing the cars of harried parents through the accumulating slush. Imagine your consternation as you look up to see two of your most trusted and reliable teachers rushing to start their cars before the first bus leaves the building.

What just happened? Well, when you told them that they could leave as soon as the students were gone, they assumed that "gone" meant "gone from the rooms." However, you assumed that they understood that "gone" meant "gone from the school property." The two teachers interpreted what you told them in the context of the fact that they were worried about their long drives home. Shaking your head, you promise yourself to be more specific next time.

Listeners interpret cues and make sense of the speaker's message in terms of their own experiences (Purdy, 1997). Strategic listeners adapt to the varied communication styles of speakers and are conscious of how meaning changes from person to person and situation to situation.

You can examine collective, shared meanings to learn the norms and assumptions that guide the decisions and actions of your faculty and staff. You can listen for how members are rewarded and the priorities that repeatedly get the group's attention. You can get additional clues about your school culture by watching to see whose presence is necessary for the group to function well and how decisions are made. If you listen for the interrelationships among the perspectives of the entire staff, you can create a new reality that everyone can understand. When you and your faculty and staff begin to listen, as a group, for collective meaning, a whole new world of possibilities opens up for the entire school.

LISTENING TO UNDERSTAND ASSUMPTIONS

Many problems with listening have to do with wrong assumptions. Quite often, people assume that words have the same meaning for everyone (Purdy, 1997). This is seldom true. As principal, you need to recognize both the differences and the similarities among your teachers' perspectives. And you need to ask appropriate questions so that each individual's unique worldview is taken into account (Brownell, 1993).

Teachers' unspoken assumptions can make or break schoolwide initiatives. Ask any principal who has announced an exciting idea to improve instruction only to have the teachers quietly sabotage the enterprise with disdain or lukewarm enthusiasm at best. The important thing to recognize is that opinions and judgments are usually based on layers of past experiences, influences, and generalizations. Consider this example.

Martha, a colleague of ours, was determined to raise test scores in her school, even though the scores were respectable by district standards. She knew that her students could do even better with more focused math instruction, so she set about trying to find the best way to teach mathematics to the students in her school. She read the research, talked to experts, and visited with principals who had successfully raised math scores in their schools. Then, with great excitement, Martha presented the research and the beginnings of a math improvement plan at a staff meeting.

The teachers at her school were hardworking professionals, and she believed they would jump on the opportunity to make a positive change in their instructional practices. To her astonishment and disappointment, every teacher at the meeting rolled his or her eyes and looked at her with varying degrees of defiance. "We're already doing that," they said as they firmly closed their minds to Martha's exciting idea. Stunned by the lack of enthusiasm, Martha went back to her office to try to understand what had happened. That afternoon, and over the next few days, she spent time talking with each classroom teacher. After spending a number of hours strategically listening, she began to uncover the assumptions that caused the resistance.

In this case, there were two unspoken assumptions in place that affected how the teachers reacted to the idea of improving math instruction in the school. First, the teachers had become accustomed to having a reputation in the school district for good test scores and did not feel that any change was needed. Second, when former principals presented new initiatives, there was little support in the way of training and follow-up for the teachers. Therefore, it was easy for them to dismiss any new idea as one that should not be taken seriously.

Assumptions are the building blocks that individuals use to make sense of the world and support mental models. By inquiring and reflecting, you can dig deeply into the matters that concern them and create breakthroughs in your ability to solve problems. In reflecting, you can identify patterns, generate new ideas, perceive common ground, and gain sensitivity to subtle meaning (Ellinor & Gerard, 1998). The more proficient you are in identifying assumptions, the more accomplished you will be in peeling them away to see what is causing the difficulty. In this way, you can enhance your listening, learning, and effectiveness. When you try to see the world through the eyes of your constituents, you acknowledge the value of your constituents' perspectives. This is a powerful act of respect and value (Ellinor & Gerard, 1998).

Most educators agree that, in spite of the many bright spots in public education, improvements and changes must be made in order to prepare students for life in the 21st century. Although changes are needed at all levels of education, the most important site is at the individual school itself. Effective principals can lead the school community by creating a vision and motivating that community to work to achieve that vision for the school.

Listening strategically to faculty, staff members, parents, and students through serious conversation and thoughtful dialogue is an important first step toward building meaningful relationships in order to take constructive action toward student success. As you read through the rest of this book, think of your own school and your own experiences.

2 The Listening Process and Different Ways We Listen

The key to success is to get out into the store and listen to what the associates have to say. It's terribly important for everyone to get involved. Our best ideas come from clerks and stockboys.

—Sam Walton

Strategic listening is more than just tuning in to sounds. Picture the husband who has one eye on *Monday Night Football* and the other eye on the newspaper while his wife tries to tell him the car sounds funny. It's only a matter of time before the exasperated wife, who normally has the patience of a saint, explodes: "You're not listening!" You know these folks. One of them might be you.

In the same way that a spouse unconsciously communicates indifference to his or her other half, you can communicate indifference to a student, teacher, custodian, or parent. Consider the teacher who comes into your office and is trying to explain how concerned she is about an impending parent conference. If you pick up a ringing phone, you are strongly communicating to the teacher that you are not seriously listening to what she has to say. At this point, you're not listening strategically.

THE PROCESS OF STRATEGIC LISTENING

Strategic listening requires, first, that you pay attention to what is being said, and second, that the speaker understands that you are doing so. There are specific ways that you can signal to a speaker that you are listening, and they frequently follow a pattern. Initially, you may demonstrate that you are interested in what is being said by making a short positive or sympathetic verbal or nonverbal gesture. You may then ask a question or make a remark to encourage the speaker to continue. You might also respond by giving feedback so the speaker knows how you interpreted what you heard, or you can simply make a comment to advance the conversation (Wolvin & Coakley, 1996).

This type of exchange can take place anywhere and at any time. Suppose you drop into the library toward the end of the school day. Ellen, the media specialist, is up to her eyeballs with volunteers who are preparing for the annual book fair. The book fair is a huge moneymaker for the Parent-Teacher Association and a big event for the school community.

When she sees you, Ellen breaks away from a group of volunteers who are energetically stocking shelves with paperback books. "What a day," she says.

You received her message, so you respond, "I can tell." This is your attending statement to signal Ellen that you are listening. "How's it going?"

"It's going," she smiles.

You glance around the room and realize that even though Ellen has made a pleasant enough comment, you would like some more information. You ask a focused question to guide her to the information that you really want. "Are you going to be ready when the sale opens this evening at 6:30?"

"We will if we could just get a few more tables up here."

You respond to Ellen with feedback to let her know how you interpreted her statement. "So that's all you need to be ready on time?"

"Yes." Ellen verifies that you understood her correctly.

"I'll have one of the custodians find more tables and set them up for you. How many do you need?" You use this question to continue the conversation and obtain even more specific information. By the time you finish the conversation, a minor problem has been solved, and Ellen knows that you support her as she coordinates an important event.

Listening can be a complicated process. How can we define something that no one can see? According to a pair of communication experts who have done extensive research on the subject, listening is "the process of receiving, attending to and assigning meaning to aural and visual stimuli" (Wolvin & Coakley, 1996, p. 69).

First, you have to be able to receive the message the speaker is trying to send to you. One of the authors experienced great frustration in trying to receive a speaker's message when she was in graduate school. It was an unseasonably warm evening, and the windows of the ground floor classroom were thrown open to catch a cool breeze. She was eager for class to start so she could hear one of her favorite professors. To this day, she can't tell you what the man talked about, but she can tell you that the rock concert on the quad severely impaired her reception of his message.

Assuming you can actually hear the message, you have to be able to pay attention to it. One of our colleagues, a principal with more than 20 years of experience, summed up his feelings about not being able to attend well to a speaker in certain situations. "It bothers me greatly when we have important conversations in the hallways, because I know that I am terribly capable of not being totally focused. Not listening, not understanding, not fully appreciating the extent of what's said. And I think sometimes teachers get distressed about it." He knew he did not listen well when he was distracted, and it concerned him.

Another important step in listening is assigning meaning to the message. Wolvin and Coakley (1996) also noted that aural and visual stimuli can strongly affect how we listen. Aural stimuli can be defined as those that are perceived with the ear. Aural stimulation includes verbal data, such as words and the sounds that make up words. Voice cues, such as increased volume or lowered pitches, are types of vocal data. Nonlinguistic data, such as the sound of a door slamming or footsteps, can also affect how we interpret what we hear.

Visual stimuli can powerfully influence how we interpret what we hear. Wolvin and Coakley (1996) reported that one researcher found that as much as 93% of total meaning or feeling in a conversation comes from nonverbal cues, or what we see rather than what we hear. What we see may include the speaker's gestures, posture, nervous mannerisms, facial expressions, and eye movement (Knapp & Hall, 2002).

An effective school leader employs visual cues to listen strategically when working with groups of constituents. One principal we know learned early in his administrative career to keep an eye on the person he called his "bellwether teacher," the teacher to whom other members of the staff tended to look when deciding how to react to new ideas. He knew that if Rachael, an accomplished and opinionated veteran teacher, smiled and nodded as he presented an idea in a faculty meeting, the idea would be readily accepted and the meeting would go well. Conversely, if Rachael shook her head, laughed sarcastically, or flushed, the principal knew he had a lot of work to do to get the rest of the faculty on board. It didn't take long for this principal to figure out that to be an effective leader, it was advantageous to discuss new ideas with Rachael and other leaders before springing them on the entire staff.

Different Ways We Listen

There are different styles of listening that have been identified by psychologists and communication experts. Any of these ways can be a part of strategic listening. Let's look at some of the most common styles in order to understand how they can affect the way we listen strategically.

Discriminative Listening

The simplest and most basic style of listening is discriminative listening. With this style, you listen in order to distinguish aural, or auditory, stimulation (Borisoff & Hahn, 1997). We use discriminative listening to detect and interpret cues that can be heard in another person's voice. One type of vocal cue is found in paralanguage, which includes pitch, the highness or lowness of sound; volume, the degree of loudness; inflection, the change in pitch or loudness; tension, the tautness of the voice; and rate, the speed of speech.

Learning to pick up vocal cues can be effective in the school setting, as the following scenario demonstrates. A principal we know received a new assignment as the administrator in a well-established school. Taking care of first things first, she managed to learn the names of everyone on the staff by the last week of August, found the most important files, approved the master schedule, and made sure the lawn was mowed.

Pleased with herself, she decided to walk the building. She encountered teachers scurrying up and down the halls from their classrooms to supply closets and back again and noticed colorful bulletin boards and tidy room arrangements slowly emerging from the chaos of those time-honored August rituals. Delighted with everyone's progress, she stepped into the classroom of an experienced teacher who had transferred from another school. With her was a much younger teacher who was also new to the school. Even though both greeted her pleasantly enough, she sensed some tension in the air. As she stood there making small talk, she noticed that both of the women were facing one another as they leaned against the same empty bookcase. They smiled tightly and spoke in short, clipped phrases as they gripped the furniture with both hands.

"So," she said when she began to realize what was going on. "I guess you've found all your books and supplies."

"Uh-huh," replied one determined lady, as the other nodded and said, "Just about everything." There was a pause. "Well, we both need a bookcase, and this is the only one left." Both looked at the principal expectantly.

"Great," the principal thought. "Tell you what. One of you take this piece of furniture, and we'll order a new one. Decide between yourselves what to do." The older teacher got the bookcase in question, the younger teacher got a new one, and the principal managed to avert a mini-crisis by using discriminative listening to listen strategically.

Vocal characterizers are another type of vocal cue. They include laughing, sighing, yawning, speech disturbances, or nonfluencies and are cues that can signal meaning to the listener. Speech disturbances can include repeated words or syllables, omissions, false starts, or slips of the tongue. Another vocal cue that can be used to interpret meaning is using syllables such as *er, uh,* or *um* to fill pauses. Any of these vocal cues can impact the way the listener interprets what is being said. A subtle yawn may communicate boredom, false starts and filler syllables may connote uncertainty, and a slip of the tongue may indicate a lack of concentration or dishonesty. However, you need to listen strategically and be cautious about reading the correct meaning into the cues.

Comprehensive Listening

Comprehensive listening is when you listen to understand the intended message (Purdy, 1997). Comprehensive listening is successful if the listener receives the message, attends to it, and assigns meaning to it that closely matches what the speaker intended (Wolvin & Coakley, 1996).

We use comprehensive listening in both our personal and professional lives. As you leave the house in the morning, you may hear your spouse reminding you of an important social engagement. You may hear a thoughtful commentary on the radio as you drive to work. A secretary may relate an incident that happened to her son at the scout meeting the night before. Teachers may stop you to chat about classroom challenges or tell stories about individual students. So it goes. You employ comprehensive listening to understand verbal messages all day long.

Sometimes, messages get mangled. One interesting phenomenon that can cause problems when we try to listen comprehensively is that we think much faster than we can talk. We can process an average of 500 words per minute in our minds but can speak at an average of only 125 to 150 words per minute. That amounts to about 400 words of extra thinking time per minute (Purdy, 1997). It shouldn't be a surprise that your mind can easily wander when you're listening to someone.

Therapeutic Listening

Therapeutic listening is another style that can be a part of strategic listening. It is a way for us to listen to someone in a supportive and nonjudgmental way (Purdy, 1997). You can use it to provide a troubled speaker with an opportunity to talk through a problem (Wolvin & Coakley, 1996). When you listen therapeutically, you

- Focus your attention on the speaker.
- Create a supportive environment.
- Listen with empathy.

To focus on the speaker, you have to find a way to eliminate or subdue auditory and visual distractions. This means that you may need to find a quiet place to talk and shut out distractions. This is not necessarily easy to accomplish on an average busy day in your office, but it's important.

Part of developing a supportive environment is exhibiting behavior that signifies that you are listening. This behavior includes how you hold your body, nod your head, and make facial expressions. It also includes an empathetic tone of voice and, perhaps, a physical gesture, if appropriate.

Consider the following difficult situation. The class you just watched Chris teach was astonishingly dreadful. It seems as though his classes are less organized every time you visit, and nothing you do seems to help. You ask him to meet you in your office after school. When he arrives, you create a supportive environment by shutting the door and asking him to join you at your small conference table. You assume a relaxed position and ask him to share his perception of what you observed.

After a couple of weak excuses, he finally admits without prompting, "It was pretty awful."

"Yes, it was," you agree quietly. You lean toward him a bit, and in a concerned voice you say, "Chris, we've been working on this all semester. What else do you need me to do to help you?"

"I don't know." His shoulders slump and he talks in a barely perceptible voice. "I really want to be a good teacher, but it's just not working." You sit quietly waiting for him to resume.

"I'm tired all the time, and sometimes I get so dizzy all I want to do is lie down someplace." He looks at you helplessly. "I don't even enjoy being around my own children anymore. I don't know what to do."

You smile and say something supportive, like "I can relate to that." Then you add, "Why don't you use my phone to call your wife to pick you up." You jot down the number of a specialist at Human Resources and hand it to him. "While you're waiting for her, call this number. We have people in the district who can direct you to almost any kind of help you need."

As you walk out the door of your office, you see Chris pick up the phone, and you know the time you spent listening strategically was time well spent. Chris is taking that important first step to getting the help he needs for his own mental health, and you can begin to make important decisions about how best to help the students in his classes.

Critical Listening

Critical listening takes place when you want to make an intelligent response to a persuasive message (Purdy, 1997). In order to make an intelligent response, you must understand and evaluate the speaker's message. You probably use critical listening as part of your regular decision-making strategies. Some examples of situations that involve critical listening include

- Interviewing job candidates.
- Meeting with teachers to select appropriate instructional materials.
- Observing teachers in order to write performance evaluations.
- Soliciting input for the annual school plan.
- Meeting with parents or patrons to discuss issues that concern them.

Listening as a Responsive Process

It's been said that listening is the single most powerful creative act one can perform. As individuals, we listen and create reality based on what we hear. Listening is "the doorway through which we allow the world to enter" (Schrange, 1989, p. 69). We frame our perspective of reality in how we listen, to what and to whom we listen, and the assumptions through which we listen (Bennis, 1997).

How we assign meaning to words we hear is very personal. We all process what we hear through perceptual filters created by our personal backgrounds, life experiences, social-cultural contexts, and everything else that makes us unique individuals (Wolvin & Coakley, 1996). Our health and physical state can affect how we perceive what we hear. So can the sharpness of our senses. Even our expectations are important, because we tend to hear what we want to hear.

Strategic listening in a conversation is an active process in which you and at least one other person take turns speaking and listening. The words you speak are in response to the words of the other person. You either agree or disagree with the statement made by the speaker. Then, you may enlarge upon the statement and prepare a response (Shotter, 1993). At the same time, the speaker actively expects some kind of response, such as agreement, sympathy, a challenge, criticism, or the like. When you are involved in a conversation, you are continuously reacting to the words and phrases that are interjected into the stream of talk. In order for each of you to understand the other person, each conversation is a negotiated, back-and-forth process (Shotter, 1993). As a school leader, you need to be especially sensitive to this as the following example illustrates.

Alex was the principal of a large school in a community that was experiencing a huge growth in population. Late in the spring, he realized that he was going to have to assign several classes to trailers the following school year. He had not yet decided which teachers would have to move outside, but the entire idea had a marked lack of universal appeal when he announced it at a faculty meeting.

The morning after the faculty meeting, Stan, a social studies teacher, dropped by Alex's office. After some initial chitchat, Stan said, "I just wanted to tell you again how much I enjoyed that inservice on learning styles you sent me to last semester."

"I'm glad you liked it. Let me know if you see anything you'd like to attend in the fall." Alex was always pleased when any of his teachers expressed an interest in professional growth.

"Sure. I'd like to get some more ideas about hands-on learning and simulations to use in my classes. You've seen the areas I've set up in my classroom in the past couple of months."

"All the time you're spending on planning is paying off. The kids seem to be really engaged in your learning centers."

"Yeah." Stan paused. "The only downside is how much room they take up. And, boy, those kids really start growing in the spring."

"I've noticed that," Alex said, realizing where the conversation was going. "It's the same thing every year. The kids just keep getting bigger and bigger as the year goes along."

"The centers and the kids themselves take up a lot of room. I can't imagine teaching my social studies program in a cramped trailer full of growing kids, can you?" He looked at Alex expectantly.

Alex sighed. "I appreciate your input, Stan. We need to have a lot more discussion with the entire staff before we decide who goes outside."

In this conversation, it took Alex several moments of speaking and listening to realize that Stan was not in the office to discuss his social studies program; he was in the office to lobby against moving into a trailer. The conversation illustrates a couple of key points. The first is that in every face-to-face interaction, there exists what can be called "concepts of partial truths" (Shotter, 1993). In other words, not everything can be presented at all times in conversations, so we make ongoing judgments about what we hear. The second is that conversations are reciprocal, chain-linked processes in which we receive partial meanings from what the speaker has offered, and, as speakers ourselves, we give part of that meaning back (Bogotch & Roy, 1997). Listening responsively to understand the negotiated meaning of conversations is one effective way to listen strategically.

Intuitive Ways of Listening

Intuitive listening is another way to listen strategically, and there are different kinds of intuitive input that affect listening. Have you ever experienced such sensations as a tingling in your ear, butterflies in your stomach, or eye twitches, or had an "ah ha!" moment when everything finally becomes clear? These are examples of intuitive input, or what some call manifestations of a hunch.

In *The Intuitive Principal*, Dyer and Corothers (2000) talk about taking environmental scans, which they define as your ability to use all of your senses to read between the lines of a situation. In addition to scanning environmental data, when you listen intuitively, you think through past experiences, such as previous encounters and prior conversations, and bring that information to bear on the current interaction.

You do this all the time. You listened intuitively when you realized that one of your custodians had a serious problem. He called in sick more and more often on Mondays, and his work was getting sloppy. He became more and more argumentative with the head custodian, and he seemed to be avoiding you. It all made sense the night you went back to your office after dinner to finish a report and found him dozing in a chair. You didn't need to smell his breath to know that he had been drinking, and it was affecting his work. Your intuition had put all the clues together for you. Intuitive listening is an important part of strategic listening.

3 Barriers to Effective Listening

If the person you are talking to doesn't appear to be listening, be patient. It may simply be that he has a small piece of fluff in his ear.

—A. A. Milne, *Winnie the Pooh*

In Chapter 2, we outlined various strategies for listening; however, strategic listening at school is often not that simple. Our days are so full of responsibility and the demands of our constituents that we can easily forget to listen well. With everything that can go wrong when we try to make sense of our school day, it's a wonder that we ever understand one another.

EMOTIONAL TRIGGERS

The long school day is ending and you have one last meeting before tackling the stack of paperwork you've ignored all afternoon. Almost every school has some version of the committee with whom you're about to meet. The staff elects representatives to get together once a month with the principal to air grievances and present problems. In some schools, the committee can be nonproductive and even unpleasant, but you're fortunate. You have a group of teachers and staff members that consistently raises legitimate concerns and is willing to discuss workable solutions.

On this particular day in October, you have no reason to believe that the impending meeting will be difficult. The school year is off to a great start, and everything you have been working for with the staff is falling into place. As committee members trail into your office, you smile to yourself and think, "What a great group." You're pleased to see your guidance counselor, three of your strongest teacher leaders, as well as a second-year teacher with tremendous leadership potential. What makes this group so special, you think, is the fact that the members are so thoughtful and supportive.

After a few moments of discussion regarding the quality of substitute teachers used recently, the special education department chair says quietly, "The teachers are exhausted."

"I know," you respond. "It's like this every year, but it's October, and things will settle down soon."

"No," another teacher pipes up. "It's different this year. We've got too much to do. It seems as though every time we turn around, you want us to do something new. Everyone is completely stressed out and morale is low."

This is not what you were expecting. Of course, they're working hard, but you are, too! You spend hours doing countless tasks. Good things for students are starting to happen, and you know that all of the demanding work is worth it.

"Tell me about some of the things that are causing stress," you say carefully. There is a knot slowly growing in your stomach, and you feel yourself start to breathe a little faster.

"Well, it's all this technology you're expecting us to use," shares the most veteran teacher in the group.

You think to yourself, "You mean the technology this school should have had in place for five years? The technology that we have now only because of the countless hours in meetings and on the phone cajoling the PTA to raise funds to buy what the students should have had anyway?"

One by one, members of the committee list their grievances. "The new reading strategies are taking up a lot of time." *The strategies aren't so new, you think darkly.*

"You expect us to spend instructional time with the students in the garden." *Most teachers would give a right arm for a learning garden like ours.*

"This year you want us to write monthly articles to post on the school Web site." *The parents love* all three paragraphs *someone on your team had to write.*

"Now we don't have time to do our lesson planning."

What? You scream silently. *No time to plan?* The knot in your stomach is becoming more pronounced and you feel your jaw tightening. *We will not stop doing what we're doing because this is what we have to do!*

Something tells you to let them talk, but you find yourself fighting the impulse to say, "I don't care how stressed you are! Do it!" Another part of you wants to declare, "Fine. Don't do it." You feel blindsided, and listening strategically is something that you are not in the mood for at the moment. The defensive surge of hurt and anger you are managing to conceal has become a serious block to listening.

For years, communication experts have studied barriers to effective listening. In 1960, Jack Gibb described some of the characteristics that speakers and listeners demonstrate in a defensive climate (Wolvin & Coakley, 1996). He described one characteristic that he called *evaluation*. You become evaluative when you judge others from your own perspective. In the situation that is taking place in your office, you know that the schoolwide initiatives teachers are complaining about are simply good practice that should have been put into place years ago. From your point of view, most teachers on the staff are quite capable of implementing the appropriate changes.

A defensive characteristic closely related to evaluation is *certainty*. Certainty can cause the listening climate to become defensive when you fail to ask teachers for input. You begin to assume that you know what is going on when, in reality, you're getting only part of the picture. In the case of what is happening in your office, you are absolutely convinced that the schoolwide initiatives are constructive. Because you see positive changes, you incorrectly imagine that the teachers are as delighted as you are.

An even stronger characteristic that a listener might unconsciously employ to create a defensive climate is that of *superiority*. This characteristic can emerge when you deliberately do not ask for advice and do not try to facilitate teamwork because you are certain that you know far more than the teachers with whom you work. Superiority started to manifest itself as you mentally listed all the hard work *you personally did* to accomplish the goals of the school.

When you thought, "I don't care how stressed you are. Do it!" you came close to exhibiting a fourth characteristic of a defensive climate, *control*. You would be hard pressed to argue that being demanding enough to think in exclamation points is not "controlling," even though you know that curtailing the opinions of the teachers and trying to coerce them to do things your way is seldom productive.

The fact is that, at this moment, the way you listen to your teachers and what you say next could have serious consequences for your initiatives and for morale in the building. If you give in to the impulses fueled by your own defensiveness and utter the self-protective thoughts spinning through your mind, you will damage the support of the individuals who trusted you by sharing their anxieties.

So, what *do* you do in a situation where you feel under attack and you are absolutely certain that you're right? You might want to look at Gibb's description of a supportive climate, which includes the following characteristics (Wolvin & Coakley, 1996):

Description: You ask members of the committee questions, without being judgmental, in order to picture what really might be causing concerns.

Problem-Orientation: You discuss their concerns and look for a solution to the problem, or you allow the teachers to find their own solutions to the problems.

Supportive: When all of you in the room are honest with one another and have no hidden agenda, your teachers will feel that you back them in what they do.

Empathy: This can be hard. You must demonstrate that you understand, even though you may not necessarily agree with what is said.

Equality: When you demonstrate equality in a conversation, you share your own ideas and show respect for the ideas of others. Many ideas that staff members conjure up can be quite amazing when thoughts start to flow.

Provisionalism: Here's the tricky one for many of us. You remain open to new ideas and accept the fact that sometimes you have to rethink and reconsider some of your own ideas.

If you're a strategic listener, and you find yourself in the hot seat in a situation that makes you feel defensive, we recommend that you do the following. Take a deep breath and firm control of your ego, and say, "I had no idea how everyone felt. Can you be specific about your concerns?" Then, settle back in your chair and listen as your colleagues pour out their frustrations. When the stream of talk finally slows down, share your reasoning for the changes and ask, "Now, what do we need to do to fix this?"

As the teachers speak and you listen, you may be reminded that, for the most part, your staff really is thoughtful and supportive. They simply needed to state their concerns in a supportive environment, and you needed to listen strategically. We can pretty much guarantee that if you use strategic listening to build a supportive climate, your team will figure out how to fix the problem.

Strategic Listening Problems

Intrapersonal and Extrapersonal

"I want to get my own way, but I want people to like it," a colleague said in a moment of candor. Most of us can relate to that comment. It's normal to want to express your own point of view and have people agree with you, especially if you're a school leader responsible for a multitude of agendas. However, it's important to remember that you have a personal frame of reference, or perspective, that acts as a filter for everything you experience. That unique frame of reference causes you to react to verbal and nonverbal messages in the way that you do.

Linguists study a fascinating phenomenon called *inner speech*, which influences individual perceptions of what is spoken. Inner speech is the silent, or subvocalized, speech used to make possible symbolic thoughts in the process of assigning meaning to words. Simply put, inner speech is the private language that you unconsciously design for yourself. This is very different from the extrapersonal, or verbal, messages that you exchange with other people. The arrangement of words in sentences, or syntax, is often compressed in inner speech, even though it may sound a bit like verbal speech. A single word can signify or refer to much more than it would at the verbal level (Johnson, 1993).

For example, when you write your agenda for the monthly staff meeting, it is usually necessary to write only single words or phrases, such as "library" or "math supplies." There is no need to make notes to yourself, because you know what you mean when you write the list. You know that "library" means that the librarian will announce the hours of circulation for the last week of school, and "math supplies" means that the math chair will ask teachers to create a list of needed books and supplies for the following year.

Your agenda would have no meaning to anyone else because your words must be elaborated on to have meaning. If you are called away on an emergency the afternoon of the meeting, your assistant principal would be clueless as to how to convey your intended message to the faculty unless you write more detailed notes (Johnson, 1993).

Quite often, short verbal exchanges using compressed speech successfully convey your intended message. For example, you might ask a teacher, "Would you chair the school technology committee this year?" Rather than replying "No, I will not chair the school technology committee this year," the teacher's response would probably be, "No," with the requisite pained expression. This shortened reply is possible because both of you understand the subject of the sentence, and it is not necessary to repeat it (Johnson, 1993).

Compressed speech can become a barrier to listening when you jump to conclusions about the meaning of what a teacher or staff member says based on your own personal shorthand. When listening strategically, it never hurts to take an extra moment to have the speaker clarify what he or she is saying. It could prevent the bruised feelings or major problems too often caused when individuals don't take the time to understand one another.

LISTENING TO OURSELVES

The fast processing of inner speech and message interpretation is both useful and hazardous. A single word in inner speech can have an array of meanings beyond those in the spoken language. Due to the inherently and structurally egocentric nature of inner speech, the meaning you give words is extremely personal. This can sometimes cause problems for you, because understanding someone else requires you to decode the message based on the *speaker's* intended meaning (Johnson, 1993).

You have to listen to yourself and acknowledge your own feelings when listening to others. If you find yourself becoming uncharacteristically annoyed by what you hear, you may be reacting to the fact that you overslept that morning or you got a ticket on the way to work. To listen strategically, you need to recognize that what you are feeling may have nothing to do with what the speaker is saying. You may need to take a break until the unreasonable feeling of irritation passes.

Inner speech greatly affects the perception of what you hear and how you hear it. As you listen, you significantly reduce the syntax of the message. It takes more than 4,000 words to expand systematically and syntactically one minute of inner speech into conversational speech (Purdy, 1997). This accounts for the estimated differences in how fast you speak and how fast you listen. All kinds of words, phrases, and thoughts constantly run through your mind, so it's important for you to be able to listen to yourself before you can listen effectively to others. Even though you're a nice person (ask anyone) with only the best of intentions, sometimes you have to fight through your own inner voices to listen strategically.

Think about the afternoon when absolutely nothing seems to be going your way. You receive a phone message from Max in Human Resources about a teacher being transferred to your school without your input. You just finished reading another one of Mrs. Anthony's scathing e-mails about the abysmal quality of her son's education, and you find the memo saying that you have to be at an IEP (Individual Educational Plan) meeting you hadn't planned on first thing in the morning. While none of these situations constitutes a crisis, you use superhuman self-control to keep from succumbing to a silent tantrum.

In pops Edna, bless her heart. The dear woman, a teacher for more than 30 years, loves to drop by every so often to chat about whatever is on her mind.

"Guess what!" she beams.

"What?" you ask obediently. *Drat.* A very bad word pops into your head. You can't go to the IEP at 9:00.

"I finished the PowerPoint." You smile broadly, because you're pretty sure that's what you're supposed to do. You remember you have a conference scheduled with Mr. Adams at exactly the same time as the meeting.

"Great." You wonder what Mr. Adams wants. He's usually pretty nice. What PowerPoint?

"Can you believe it?" Maybe someone else can go to the IEP. Edna looks at you expectantly.

"Of course I can," you say gamely. "What's not to believe?" Who the heck does Mrs. Anthony think she is? And who, by the way, gave Human Resources the right to plop anyone they want to in this school?

"Meredith helped me," Edna says, clearly expecting a more enthusiastic response.

Then, before you completely lose contact with reality, it hits you. Edna was the teacher who slipped out of the first staff meeting of the year in tears when you announced that all teachers would be required to create at least one multimedia presentation to use with students before the year was over.

Edna created a PowerPoint presentation! This is huge!

It's obviously time to focus on Edna. You can send a designee to the IEP conference and Mr. Adams will tell you in his own quiet way what is on his mind. You have time to compose a reply to Human Resources, even though they really do have the right to place teachers in certain situations whether you like it or not. And, to paraphrase Rick's immortal words in *Casablanca,* you'll *always* have Mrs. Anthony. Maybe you'd better do some strategic listening and help Edna celebrate her success.

"Tell me all about it," you say as you push back from your desk. "I can't wait to see the presentation." By focusing your thoughts on Edna and listening strategically to her, you know she will be taking more risks with technology in the future, and her classes will be better for it.

LISTENING FOR POINT OF VIEW

The ability to differentiate your own point of view from the point of view of another is called *decentering.* By decentering, you can assume the perspective of the thought processes of the speaker and better understand where he or she is "coming from" (Johnson, 1993).

It is the nature of interpersonal listening to make sense of the message in terms of our own personal history, intelligence, gender, age, and culture. The more varied experiences you have, the better you can understand the experiences of others. If the speaker is extremely self-centered, you will have to try to assume the speaker's perspective in order to understand his or her message. This can be time-consuming and requires a great deal of patience (Purdy, 1997).

F. J. Rothlesberger (1995), a psychologist, wrote that language and words have two main functions. The first is the *logico-experimental function*, which exists when people engage in a discussion about things they know. To engage in the logico-experimental function, the speaker and listener have a common background and share common knowledge.

An example of this might be when Amy, an experienced American history teacher, stops by to ask about the possibility of having a Colonial Festival late in the semester. You both know that a study of the original 13 colonies is part of the history curriculum, and, with proper planning, the event would be very appropriate for students at your school.

You can refer to the district's curriculum guide to make certain that the Colonial Festival is planned to stay within the boundaries of the curriculum, and you can refer to school district regulations to keep the event in proper proportion to its learning value. Any minor misunderstanding the two of you might have in planning the occasion can easily be cleared up, because either of you can refer to the curriculum guide or district regulations in order to clarify what you are trying to do.

However, people spend only a small fraction of their time in this kind of conversation. A more common conversational exchange involves the *emotive function* (Rothlesberger, 1995). Confusion can arise because people often think they are being logical when, in reality, they are basing their opinions on emotions. Therefore, social conversation is frequently an interaction of sentiments rather than facts.

For example, suppose that same American history teacher has just transferred to your school from another district. In her former position, she planned a Colonial Festival that lasted several days, culminating in a feast paid for by the school and catered by a restaurant that specialized in authentic early American cuisine. You, on the other hand, assume that she is planning an event that will last a single day. You discover by accident that she intends to create a 3-day extravaganza. She becomes angry and hurt when you tell her that she has to scale the event back to one day and that parent volunteers will supply the food. From your perspective, you are simply being practical. From the teacher's perspective, you are not being supportive of her instructional program.

Many personal sentiments are expressed in conversations that have little or no meaning apart from the personal circumstance of the person who makes them. If you have not experienced life in the same way as the speaker and you refer to words in a different or wrong context, there is likely to be a misunderstanding (Rothlesberger, 1995). Listening strategically can help prevent you from misconstruing the intent of the message.

MISUNDERSTANDINGS

There are a number of ways language can be misunderstood. We all have our own personal words to describe things (Purdy, 1997). For example, if you pack a lunch to take with you to work, you may put it in a *bag* or a *sack*. The choice of the word would depend on what part of the country you are from or how the word is used in your own family.

The meaning of words can change from situation to situation or from one subcultural group to another (Purdy, 1997). Those of us who have been around for a while begin to notice that the meaning of words can evolve with time. Words that might have been quite shocking to hear in society 30 years ago are the norm of many young people today. Sit in the student section, or even the parent section if you're over 50, of a high school football game, and you'll see what we mean.

Misunderstandings spring up when the speaker's intended message becomes distorted. If you receive a second- or third-hand verbal communication, you may well need to go back to the originator of the message to make sure you understand it the way it was intended. The more people the message goes through, the more proportionally the message gets distorted (Purdy, 1997). This happens because some details get left out and other details are added to make sense of the information that is passed on. To experience fewer listening problems having to do with language, Purdy (1997) suggests that you focus on the intended meaning, determined by the people and the situation, and ask questions when something doesn't make sense.

NONVERBAL MESSAGES

How often has a teacher walked into your office and you knew, without either of you saying a word, that you needed to shut the door to talk? How did you know that you should gesture to a chair so she could sit down? What made you think that you should wait a moment before speaking? You knew to do those things because her walk, the expression on her face, and the look in her eyes told you that she had bad news and that she needed you to listen. You both communicated nonverbally before even one word was spoken.

Listening with your eyes can be crucial for a school leader, because what you *see* can have a tremendous impact on the significance of what you *hear.* Up to 55% of the meaning you derive from a message comes from facial cues (Wolvin & Coakley, 1996). A person's face reveals how he or she feels, and the person's body reveals the intensity of the message. A strategic listener can learn a great deal by watching, because nonverbal communication is less well controlled than verbal communication. There are a number of ways that nonverbal exchanges can enhance communication and make a speaker's message clearer.

When you see people shake or nod their heads, they are *complementing the message* and affirming with their gestures that they agree or disagree with you.

On the other hand, nonverbal language can *contradict the verbal message.* If a troublesome student smirks when she says she's sorry, you know she didn't mean what she said.

Often, a nonverbal gesture can be used to *replace a verbal message,* as when the furnace repairman shrugs when you ask him how long you will be without heat.

Nonverbal gestures can also be used to *emphasize verbal messages.* When you see a normally calm teacher shaking her finger at a student as she speaks through clenched teeth, you know that she is angry.

Simply gesturing toward a chair as you invite someone to sit down is a type of nonverbal act that *repeats your spoken message* (Wolvin & Coakley, 1996).

Wolvin and Coakley (1996) write that nonverbal communication can be very informative, but it should always be interpreted with care. This is because nonverbal behavior can have a number of possible meanings. You need to look at the cultural context of the message, the relationship between those communicating, and whether the nonverbal act is perceived as deliberate or not. Each person has his or her own set of nonverbal behaviors, and the better you know someone, the easier it is to read his or her nonverbal behavior. It would be comforting to know that your financial secretary is not rubbing her forehead because you went over the textbook budget; it just makes her head feel good.

Those who are accomplished at decoding the meaning of nonverbal behavior are perceived positively by those with whom they work. They seem to be better adjusted, more extroverted, and more encouraging, as well as being warmer and more empathetic. They even seem less hostile and less manipulative (Knapp & Hall, 2002), and heaven knows we'd all like to look a little less calculating at times.

Body Language

For the past few years, the importance of understanding body language has been written about extensively in the popular press. The notion that you can understand what people think or feel simply by observing the way they sit or fold their arms is almost irresistible. The whole idea seems to have taken on an almost mystical quality, much like mind reading or clairvoyance. However, communication researchers in the field of kinesics study the language of the body and face. While kinesics can hardly be considered magical, it can provide valuable insights to school leaders intent on listening carefully to those around them. One of our colleagues calls this "listening with my eyes."

Nonverbal Actions

Ekman and Friesan (in Wolvin & Coakley, 1996) classified five nonverbal actions that can influence communication. *Emblems* are gestures that directly translate what you say verbally. They are intentional and are usually produced with your hands. You might wag your fingers toward yourself to tell a dawdling student to "come here" or cover your ears with your hands to indicate to the young ladies in the second floor restroom that they are speaking too loudly.

You use *illustrators,* actions that are directly tied to the verbal content of your message, to punctuate, clarify, or accent what you say. You might nod your head in the direction of the basketball court to point out a specific student, or you may move your hands in circles to indicate that you are searching for words to illustrate what you are trying to articulate.

Speakers might use *regulators* to control or sustain conversations. For example, a teacher might signal that she needs to end the conversation you are having at the end of the day by taking out her car keys. Another teacher with whom you are speaking might stand in the doorway of his classroom to subtly block the door in order to keep the conversation going (Wolvin & Coakley, 1996).

On the other hand, you might rub your forehead or pick at a hangnail and mean absolutely nothing at all. These gestures, called *adaptors,* are done out of habit and are seldom calculated.

Proximics is the study of the use of personal space. Most of us who are native to North America need a lot of space. Typically, we are comfortable with about two to three feet of space around us. We seem to need more personal space as we get older, and we tend to allow individuals with higher status more personal space. You may notice that men engage in more self-disclosure if you give them a lot of room, but women are sometimes more comfortable sharing personal thoughts if they sit or stand at a closer distance (Wolvin & Coakley, 1996).

Body Postures

Quite often, you can read the mood of individuals if you observe how they sit or stand. In their book *Listening,* Wolvin and Coakley (1996) describe categories of body postures that consciously or unconsciously give clues as to what individuals might be thinking or feeling. Some of those categories include

- Body orientation
- Open or closed body position
- Trunk lean
- Gestures
- Head nodding

When communication experts talk about the *orientation of one's body* in a conversation, they are discussing the extent to which we turn our shoulders and legs toward or away from another person. In general, the more we like people, the more we turn toward them when we speak. Women are much more comfortable facing one another during conversations than men are. In fact, school leaders of both genders find that many of their most productive conversations with male teachers and colleagues take place shoulder to shoulder rather than face to face.

The *open or closed body position* is demonstrated through the use of our knees and legs. When we exhibit open positions, our bodies are oriented toward the persons with whom we are talking and, if we are sitting, our legs are stretched out in front of us. Men are more likely than women to sit in this relaxed way, but people in general have more relaxed postures when interacting with friends or colleagues they like.

The *trunk lean* is a posture that communicates different things to different people. Women communicate concern for others by leaning forward, but men frequently use that posture to communicate a threat. Men are more apt to use a sideways lean to communicate ease, friendliness, and warmth. When women lean forward in a meeting situation with men, the men may respond by shutting down, changing the subject, or passing the conversation along to another participant in the meeting.

Arm and hand *gestures* can tell us even more. Even though men gesture as much as women, women tend to gesture more rapidly than men. A person with still hands is perceived as warmer than one with drumming fingers. Fiddling with a lock of hair, pulling at an eyebrow, or playing with something in your hands while you are in conference with a school board member may be perceived as nervous gestures that make you look worried or less than self-assured.

Head nodding is perceived by most of us as affirmation of what we are saying or hearing. Head nodding between two women who are interacting can mean that one is seeking approval from the other and the other is giving it. It can also mean that the woman who is listening is communicating, "I hear you." Head nodding between men usually means that they are in agreement. A woman nodding her head to communicate, "I hear you, keep going" can be misunderstood by a man to be saying, "I agree with everything you just said." When you nod your head during a conversation, people probably think of you as warm and open-minded and that you approve of what they are saying.

Facial Gestures

Your face can be very communicative. It expresses emotions and reflects your level of interest in the conversation. Your face can show multiple emotions or what are called *affect blends* (Wolvin & Coakley, 1996). For example, you might be showing happiness in a smile, but be showing anger or frustration with raised eyebrows. Your eyes tell a story as well. The more you look at the face of your partner in conversation, the more you are perceived as being attentive, empathetic, and positive (Wolvin & Coakley, 1996).

Matching and Closeness

Interaction synchrony is matching behavior that often occurs during open and friendly conversations. We tend to unconsciously mimic the gestures, postures, and facial expressions of the persons with whom we are interacting positively. You can put another at ease by matching his or her gestures or facial expressions. It might be a sign of a positive conversation if you find yourself crossing your legs or folding your arms in the same manner as the parent sitting across from you in a long conference (Knapp & Hall, 2002).

Immediacy actions are behaviors that signal closeness between two people (Knapp & Hall, 2002). These behaviors include

- More forward lean
- Closer proximity
- More eye contact
- More direct body orientation

- More relaxed posture
- More positive facial expressions

Being alert for these signals can help us monitor the success of a conversation. However, they are not foolproof. Two people present at the same event can interpret another person's postures or gestures very differently—as demonstrated in the different ways in which men and women can interpret body orientation or head nodding. The manner in which we construe experiences is influenced by our culture, education, or experiences. Sometimes, our moods can bias what we see in another person's face, and we tend to see what we want to see rather than what is really happening (Knapp & Hall, 2002). Although nonverbal language and body language can provide valuable clues to facilitate strategic listening, we need to be careful not to read too much into nonverbal and body language when we try to understand the other person.

COMMUNICATION DIFFERENCES

Cultural Differences

Most of us are leaders in schools that are marked by changing demographics. Because of transforming patterns of immigration and other factors too numerous to mention here, many of our schools look different now from how they did a few years ago. Some schools have students who speak one of as many as 100 different primary languages. Even the small number of predominantly white, middle-class communities that still exist now have, at the very minimum, a handful of students who are English language learners.

Although our greatest concern is how to listen strategically to, and communicate with, students and parents who speak languages other than English, we need to be aware that the different cultures in which we grow up greatly influence how we interpret the messages we receive from those around us. When individuals from two different cultures speak, there may be two different behavioral norms in evidence, and it's very likely that there may be two different worldviews selectively screening information (Thomlinson, 1997).

Culture is "the set of customs, behaviors, beliefs, and language that distinguish a particular group of people and make up the background, experience, and perceptual filters of individuals within that group" (Wolvin & Coakley, 1996, p. 124). Values and beliefs determine what we consider "right" and how things ought to be done.

We all have values and beliefs that influence the way we listen to others. In the United States, we are brought up to believe that everyone should have the same opportunity to be successful. Opportunity and equality are considered to be virtues and worthy ideals. Because of this ingrained belief in equality, we tend to relate to others in a comparatively informal way. We can be more casual in our conversations, greetings, and clothing than people of many other cultures. Sometimes, our lack of deference for position and status can be interpreted as a lack of respect. As strategic listeners, when interacting with people from different cultures, we need to show respect by interpreting cues and not being overly familiar. We need to listen to introductions and greetings and respond appropriately (Thomlinson, 1997).

In our U.S. culture, most of us prefer a direct approach when we deal with one another. We don't like someone to "beat around the bush" or "skirt the issue" when he or she has something to say to us. Even if the message is painful, we generally want people to get to the point so we can make sense of the situation and determine how best to react. This behavior can cause people from other cultures to assume that Americans are less patient and less willing to listen than people in other parts of the world. Our culture tends to put far more emphasis on speaking than on listening (Thomlinson, 1997).

Americans tend to be viewed by people of other cultures as assertive, talkative, and extroverted. We value time and punctuality highly and consider goal setting and getting down to business important. When listening to individuals from other cultures, we need to remember that the *relationship* between two speakers is often as important as the *words* that are spoken. In other cultures, people are often expected to talk about family and other interests because they are valued highly. Time, too, can be valued very differently in other cultures (Thomlinson, 1997).

We need to listen to ourselves for words or gestures that would appear to be aggressive or antagonistic to people from other cultures (Thomlinson, 1997). We value individualism and personal accomplishment and encourage competition. For most of us, it is an honor to be singled out for recognition; we perceive it as a sign of respect. Many people from the Middle East, Africa, and Asia are embarrassed to be singled out for an honor. In Japan, for example, praise can be considered an insult, because the group is more important than the individual. As a member of a group, if you praise someone, you are, in effect, boasting about yourself (Tannen, 1998).

So, what does all of this have to do with strategic listening during the school day? Because we have more students, parents, and teachers who come to us from different cultures, we need to be sensitive to how people of different cultures perceive and process information. For example, we should be slow to criticize parents from Hispanic cultures who arrive late to conferences or programs, because they may have not yet learned that in the United States, we almost always begin at the announced time. We should be sensitive to the fact that parents and teachers from Asian countries are taught to value harmony and may be hesitant to discuss issues and concerns as directly as those of us raised in the United States.

What is considered strategic listening in one culture could be misunderstood or be considered inappropriate in another culture. We need to understand that, in our own culture, we have our own ways of speaking that color our assumptions and shape the way we think. However, strategic listening can take place in any culture; people from nearly every culture appreciate listeners who demonstrate empathy and understanding in their interactions with others (Wolvin & Coakley, 1996).

Religious Differences

The courts have made it clear that there is little place in our public schools for organized religion. However, we need to remember that no matter what faith, if any, we profess, our beliefs can still color the way we think and operate at school. These beliefs can surface in very different ways. For example, at one school we know of, the faculty enjoyed an annual Thanksgiving potluck luncheon. Because of the significance of the occasion, it was expected that someone would lead an ecumenical prayer of thanks. This worked very nicely until the year that one of the teachers, a part-time youth minister at a local evangelical church, automatically ended a lovely prayer with the phrase "in Jesus' name we pray." After the principal spent the evening calling Jewish members of the staff to apologize, he and the faculty decided that a Thanksgiving poem might be more appropriate for the following year.

The Thanksgiving prayer is a blatant and embarrassing illustration of how innocently we can offend one another due to religious beliefs, but we can hurt one another in more subtle ways. A vocal music teacher can include music from every religion and culture in the winter concert and still accidentally leave out songs that are important to some members of the audience. An open-minded teacher can make a statement equating church, synagogue, or mosque affiliation with ethical values and offend a morally upright agnostic colleague. As strategic listeners, we must continue to be sensitive to the fact that everyone has closely held beliefs to which we need to be alert and to respect.

Gender-Based Differences

In the musical *My Fair Lady*, Professor Henry Higgins accepts the challenge of teaching Eliza Doolittle, a cockney flower girl, to speak with an upper-class British accent. Although his experiment succeeds beyond anyone's imagination but his own, he becomes frustrated with Eliza's seemingly illogical behavior. In one of the production's most entertaining numbers, an exasperated Higgins implores the audience to answer the question, "Why can't a woman be more like a man?" It is painfully obvious to everyone but Higgins that Eliza isn't irrational; the two of them speak to and listen to one another in two similar but very different languages.

Although usually not as dramatic as characters on a Broadway stage, a school leader's ability to make sense of what is going on can be made more complex by gender differences in listening styles. Female principals in conversation with male teachers or male principals in conversation with female teachers may find themselves frustrated when what they hear is not at all what the teacher intended to communicate. Principals need to take gender differences into account when listening to their teachers.

Deborah Tannen (1990), in *You Just Don't Understand: Men and Women in Conversation*, writes that misunderstandings between men and women in conversation often occur because the genders have different conversational rituals. Men use put-downs, jokes, and bantering to gain the one-up position in an interchange. Tannen (1990) uses the phrase *one-up* to refer to men's need to dominate a hierarchical relationship. Women tend to endeavor to sustain a semblance of equality in a conversation. They take into account how the listener might feel about what is being said and downplay their own influence in order to achieve a goal.

Tannen (1990) addressed the age-old frustration between men and women regarding asking directions. Men generally are not inclined to ask for directions or to ask any kinds of questions in front of others. In their perception, to reveal a lack of knowledge is to become one-down, or less dominant, in the eye of others. On the other hand, women usually have no fear of asking for directions or asking questions. Unfortunately, in work situations, women are generally unaware that asking questions is perceived by men to be revealing ignorance in front of others and may create a negative impression.

One of us was made aware of this many years ago when she was assigned an earnest young teacher named Steve to work with her as her administrative intern in summer school. Steve, a youthful, aspiring administrator, was determined to do his job perfectly and to begin his ascent to superintendency on the right foot.

No one could have worked harder or longer than Steve. It took him two weeks to give up wearing a crisply starched shirt and snappy silk tie, even when cleaning out the bookroom on a sweltering summer day. Steve was respectful of the author as she directed summer school and taught him what she knew about being a principal, but one day Steve was so appalled by something that happened that he challenged her, in private, to explain why she handled a situation in the way she did.

Because summer school took place only in the mornings, the author decided to save instructional time by having bag lunches delivered to each classroom so students could continue their academics while they ate. After consulting with officials in the central kitchen, she announced to the summer school staff that the procedure would start the following Monday morning. However, late the preceding Friday afternoon, she received a message that, for reasons that have long since been forgotten, lunches could not be delivered to classrooms until Tuesday.

Without giving it much more thought than, "Darn it," the author called a quick staff meeting before school on Monday morning to explain the change in plans. She ended the meeting by saying, "I'm sorry about the change." By the time the author made it back to her office, Steve was beside himself with righteous indignation. "Why did you tell them you were sorry? It wasn't your fault!"

Gender differences can block shared meaning in almost any situation (Borisoff & Hahn, 1997). Generally speaking, women tend to listen as much to feelings as to words. They find closeness among themselves by discussing their feelings. They desire reciprocity and disclosure from their partners in conversation. In contrast, men are more likely to listen to and discuss facts.

Gender differences may influence interpretation of what people hear in other ways (Borisoff & Hahn, 1997). Women demonstrate more nonverbal cues and are more adept at decoding the nonverbal cues of others. However, this does not necessarily indicate better listening. While men and women may hear the same message, they may listen differently. Women are socialized to listen for feelings in the process as a way of demonstrating empathy. Men offer solutions as a demonstration of empathetic listening.

Sally Helgesen (1990) found women to be more intense, thoughtful, and tentative in their listening. Women are apt to value listening as a way of making others feel comfortable and a means of encouraging them. She postulated that there is a female talent for raising others up and drawing them out. In a later book, *The Web of Inclusion*, Helgesen (1995) expressed her surprise that many men had become open to this style as the traditional way of doing things became less productive in many cases.

It is important to know that research shows that men and women often communicate differently. You can learn more when you listen to women constituents if you remember that women are likely to discuss feelings and are more comfortable with mutual give-and-take in conversations. Conversely, you will likely learn more when listening to male constituents if you remember that men tend to feel more at ease in sticking to facts. This knowledge becomes even more important when male principals listen to females and female principals listen to males. Strategic listening means that you need to be conscious of gender differences when you listen in order to hear what your teachers, staff, students, and parents mean when they speak.

Part II

Strategic Listening in Practice

4 Strategic Listening in Difficult Situations

Easy listening exists only on the radio.

—David Barkan

Overall, the best strategic listeners are those who are consistently able to read their audiences. Using that aptitude, that foundation, they diagnose people's inclinations and the logical content of their thoughts, needs, and wants. Then, they act on what they've read in both verbal and nonverbal prompts. This chapter looks at problematic areas that have an impact on your ability to listen strategically and lead effectively.

LISTENING IN A NONLINEAR CULTURE

If you examine traditional textbook management/administrative theory, you will find that researchers describe real-time practice as *linear*. Practice that is characterized by linear conditions is normally *tightly structured* and lends itself to a *routine* level of competence and performance—situations

Table 4.1   Comparing Linear Situations to Nonlinear Situations

Linear Situations (Attentive Listening Environment)	Nonlinear Situations (Strategic Listening Environment)
Discrete goals	Multiple and competing goals
Easily measured outcomes	Difficult-to-measure outcomes
Single solution to problems	Multiple and competing solutions
Structured tasks	Unstructured tasks
Steady, predictable environment	Dynamic environment
Tight management connections	Loose management connections
Indisputable operating procedures	Loosely defined operating procedures
Certain consequences of actions	Indeterminate consequences of actions
Clear lines of authority	Unclear and competing lines of authority

that require, for the most part, little more than discriminative listening. However, in the school setting in which we work, traditional management/ administrative theory is of somewhat limited value.

Education leadership is characterized by *nonlinear* conditions and, by the very nature of the situation, is *loosely structured.* Your efforts to bring about effectiveness and an extraordinary commitment to performance require strategic listening. The only things that are even close to being linear in the school environment are routine administrative tasks such as purchasing, submitting work orders, scheduling recess or classes, developing bus routes, and so forth—activities in which interactions with other people are simple, incremental, or nonexistent. If you compare theory with practice—the tightly structured linear situations of theory with your dynamic nonlinear environment—the difference is clear.

As you look at Table 4.1, which compares typical linear situations with your nonlinear school environment, take note of the relatively easy listening requirements inherent in linear situations when compared to the strategic listening requirements intrinsic in your school environment.

The majority of human interactions that take place in your school are nonlinear. Gleick (1988) noted that "nonlinearity means that the act of playing the game has a way of changing the rules" (p. 119). As an education leader, you have learned how to routinize your work as much as possible. As well as employing situational management and leadership techniques, you have probably learned the effectiveness of practicing pattern rationality. Effective leadership, where the bulk of your working environment is nonlinear, requires quick thinking and strategic listening. You need constantly to test what is happening against what you know and to act in linear ways regardless of the nonlinear environment that surrounds you.

LISTENING FOR CONFLICT MANAGEMENT AND RESOLUTION

School leaders spend a significant amount of time managing conflicts and resolving problems. Because emotions can run high in conflict situations, when you meet with people who have disagreements with you or among themselves, you may find the following techniques useful in managing the interactions effectively:

- Although you might be more interested in getting things moving your way than you are in listening to what the speaker actually has to say, pay close attention to the speaker and maintain eye contact.
- Show that you're interested. Encourage the speaker by unobtrusively confirming you are listening by using verbal cues, such as "Yes," "I see," "uh-huh." And use positive nonverbal cues at appropriate points, such as nods, smiles, or a furrowed brow.
- Lean, just slightly, toward the speaker while keeping an open, relaxed posture. Keep your physical movements to a minimum.
- Say little. You can't listen when you're talking, and you don't want to interrupt the speaker's flow.
- Engage the speaker by looking for opportunities to subtly mirror his or her cues. Don't mimic, but rather look for ways to complement the speaker's meaning and tone.
- Don't hesitate to draw the speaker out by making a statement or asking a question, such as "I'd like to hear more about that" or "I don't understand. Can you restate what you just said?"
- Listen carefully for what is not being said, what's missing.
- Observe how things are said: The emotions and attitudes behind the words may be more important than the words themselves. Much information is revealed in voice intonation, changes in volume, and body language.
- If there are other people in the room, keep them in view so you can observe their reactions to the speaker and use those observations to refine your understanding of the speaker's message.

The techniques listed above are basic effective listening techniques. Now, let's look at some more strategic conflict management and conflict resolution skills: asking questions, providing feedback, reframing, and summarizing.

Questioning

Questions serve three purposes: (a) to actively demonstrate that you're listening, especially in the early trust-building stage; (b) to gather and organize information, particularly in the problem-solving stage; and (c) to express, in question form, what otherwise might be an academic statement—to test reality, especially in problem-solving and closure stages.

Generally, your questions to the speaker should be open-ended, not closed-ended. Closed-ended questions are those that the speaker can respond to by stating a simple "yes" or "no" or with a specific answer, like "23" or "April 17th." Such questions may actually encourage the speaker to stop talking. Open-ended questions, on the other hand, can't be answered so simply and encourage the speaker to talk and explain in complete sentences. Open-ended questions invite the speaker to open up and really tell the story. Some examples of open-ended questions include statements like "Tell me more about that particular idea," "What happened next?" "How did you feel when that happened?" and "What would you like to see as an outcome?" Use open-ended questions carefully—only to increase control over the flow of information or to confirm important facts.

Feedback

Providing feedback serves as a perception check for you and a form of validation for the speaker. When the speaker pauses, there's an opportunity for you to confirm that you've been listening and that you understand by feeding back to the speaker what you've heard or observed. It's also a way to check whether your perception of what you think you heard or observed is accurate. Moreover, it's a way for you to validate the speaker's feelings. When you give feedback, repeat or paraphrase what the speaker has said or displayed as unspoken feelings. Be conscious of particular words or phrases that seem important to the speaker and use them, if appropriate, in your paraphrasing; for example, "What I think I'm hearing is that you really want to . . . " or "I can see that you have strong feelings about arts integration in the curriculum." Pause to let the speaker react to your feedback.

Reframing

Reframing is a special way of feeding back and is one of the conflict manager's most important tools. Reframing is restating what the speaker has said to capture the idea, remove negative overtones, and move the process forward. Reframing helps translate a personal statement into a statement of interests or needs. For example, suppose the speaker said, "This school bus driver is so irresponsible and stupid that I can never depend on her to pick up my child on any kind of logical schedule." Simple feedback might be, "So, it really bothers you if she's not on time to pick up Billy," while a reframed feedback might be, "So, a regular schedule is important for you and Billy." Either response may be appropriate, and the difference is subtle. The first response, simple feedback, might be better at an earlier point in trust building, whereas the second response, reframed, might be better later, during problem solving.

Summarizing

At major shifts, such as when one speaker has told his or her story but before you turn to another speaker or state your own view, you can summarize the major points and ask for confirmation. Summarizing is most effective when you use neutral language. For example, if the speaker used the words "hysterical" or "liar" in presenting his or her position, you might summarize by describing the person as one who "disagreed" or "sees things differently." However, you don't want to sound so pretentious that the speaker feels you're misrepresenting his or her point of view.

Managing the flow of communication is a conflict manager's most important tool. Central to effective strategic listening for conflict management and resolution is the ability to listen in a nonjudgmental way—to listen for understanding first and agreement later. You may want to push on to something else, but stick to the speaker's subject and give the speaker time to finish. Remember, repetition may indicate that the subject is very important to the speaker or that the speaker needs to feel that you really heard him or her. This is a cue that you might want to feed back what the speaker is saying.

Strategic listening for conflict management and resolution is a skill you need to develop and practice. While learning to listen strategically for conflict management and resolution, you may make mistakes, and you might find the techniques discussed above awkward and unnatural at first. As you practice, here are some common mistakes you need to *avoid*:

- *Parroting:* Simply repeating the message or responding only to the facts and not the feelings
- *Listening Without Empathy:* Continuing whatever activity you were involved in, not looking at the speaker, maintaining a dry detached manner
- *Philosophizing:* Using reflective thinking when the speaker needs specific help or information you possess
- *Analyzing:* Going beyond the message the speaker wants you to hear and know by adding your guess as to why the speaker feels the way he or she does
- *Cutting off:* Pushing the speaker to the "bottom line" too early

LISTENING FROM A DISTANCE:
TELEPHONE, LETTERS, NOTES, AND E-MAIL

In a previous book, Dunklee (1999) tells the story of a parent (Mrs. Roberts) with whom a principal (Sterling) had dozens of telephone conversations over a period of about 5 months. Each call had to do with problems with Mrs. Roberts' daughter, Kelly. One afternoon, Sterling called Mrs. Roberts, just to let her know that things were finally "looking up" and to reassure her that by working together, they were on the path to getting Kelly to "see the light." He mentioned to Mrs. Roberts that they had never met face-to-face and invited her to stop by the school for coffee some time. A few days later, Sterling's secretary told him that Mrs. Roberts was in the office and would like to meet him.

"Mrs. Roberts," he said, "I'm Grant Sterling. How nice of you to stop by—we finally get to meet face-to-face!"

Mrs. Roberts eyed Sterling with a puzzled look. "You're the principal? You're Mr. Sterling? I, ah, well, you know . . . you sound . . . well, you sound much *taller* on the telephone!"

Dunklee describes Sterling's height as 5 feet, 6 inches.

Although you may think of listening primarily in terms of face-to-face conversations, you spend much of your time on the job interacting with, and listening to, other people in non-face-to-face situations. Welcome to the ever-growing world of virtual communications. When you've never met the speaker but you're listening to his or her voice on the telephone or reading his or her words in letters, notes, or e-mails, you're an *online listener*. When you hear only a voice on the telephone, or hear yourself interpreting written words in your mind, you have a tendency to develop immediate assumptions about others and their intentions. As an online listener, you imagine the person behind the voice and the words—and you risk assuming or presuming too much.

An e-mail message is a communication piece directed and delivered to you in an inanimate voice format—as a "digital/virtual presence" in your mind. Try, for example, reading the e-mail message received by hypothetical Sunnyside School principal, Tom Smith, below, without developing immediate assumptions.

TSmith@sunnyside.middleschool.edu

Subject line "Request for Assistance"

Principal Smith: I am Mrs. Markem Curtis, mother of Amy Curtis, an incoming seventh grader at your school.

We are very concerned about ensuring that Amy gets not only a good education, but also an education that is right. Her father (Markem) and I wish to request your assistance in helping us ensure that Amy is not subjected to any testing that might be used to determine her psychological needs or her feelings toward her personal or family life. In addition, any outside-of-classroom testing, evaluations, or meetings with school counselors, psychologists, or social workers do not meet with our approval. Also, we are quite concerned that Amy not be involved in the discussion of morals or values, in genealogical research, or in sensitivity activities.

Please inform Amy's teachers of our desires and assure them that we are ready to assist them in any way. To ensure that we, your school, and its teachers are working together in Amy's best interests, we would like for you to require your teachers to provide us with copies of any materials, outside of the textbooks, that they will be using in class. We would like to have such materials at least 1 week in advance. Finally, we are aware public schools include exposure to different kinds of religions in their curriculum, and that your school library provides teachers with videotapes and movies concerning other areas of our society that we do not wish to have Amy exposed to. We have visited your school's library (media center), and have talked with your media specialist. We are mailing you a list of tapes, movies, books, and other print material you have in your library, or that teachers will be using in their classrooms, that Amy may not be exposed to without our express permission. In addition, we will be including some articles from a publication that we subscribe to that you may find inspiring.

Finally, if we object to any of the materials that Amy will be exposed to, we do not give permission for Amy to be removed from that class or class period. We have been advised by our church that our rights in this matter, insisting that any material we object to on Amy's behalf be removed from the curriculum, have been given us through the United States Supreme Court.

We sincerely hope that we can work together on this matter, and that Amy's education will be a cooperative one between you, Amy's teachers, and us. If you have any questions you can contact at: Curtis9@ hearmenow.net, or by phone 753-555-1212.

If you are Tom Smith, when you read the e-mail from Mrs. Curtis, you might have the urge to respond by simply saying, "No way!" However, you can't, and you can't just delete the message. Politically, you're stuck; you have to respond. You heard the Curtis message. It spoke to you, got your attention. It evoked an image, got your emotions flowing. You may not like what you heard, but we're betting that you'll read the e-mail at least two times, and it will still speak to you in the same voice.

Freud (1927) asked the question, "How does a thing become conscious . . . how does a thing become pre-conscious? And the answer would be: by coming into contact with the verbal images that correspond to it" (p. 47). One attribute of e-mail that most distinguishes it from other forms of communication is its ability to evoke images and emotion in the recipient. It's easy to get caught in the trap of impulsively firing off a hasty response. Don't! Unlike telephone or personal conversations, impulsive e-mail responses can be printed out and circulated, easily acquiring a level of importance that you never wanted or intended.

Part of any school leader's time (including days, nights, weekends, and even vacation time) is spent corresponding with constituents, peers, and bosses by phone, letters, notes, and e-mail. Non-face-to-face communication is a rapidly expanding way of life that, in spite of its handiness, has distorted public service. People expect an instant response. They get it, and it just encourages more. You need to manage your time and listening abilities to include it, and understand that it's just part of your job as a community leader.

LISTENING TO LIES

Mark Twain (1882) wrote,

> Observe, I do not mean to suggest that the custom of lying has suffered any decay or interruption—no, for the lie is a virtue, a principle that is eternal. The lie, as a recreation, a solace, a refuge in time of need, the fourth Grace, the tenth Muse, man's best and surest friend, is immortal, cannot perish from the earth while this club remains. My complaint simply concerns the decay of the art of lying. No high-minded man, no man of feeling, can contemplate the lumbering and slovenly lying of the present without grieving to see a noble art so prostituted.

There are some people who can't tell a lie and many who can't tell the truth, and, unfortunately, most people can't tell the difference. People who lie to you do so for one or more of the following basic reasons. (Feel free to add any we've missed that you've experienced.) People lie because they

- Are good at it and it's part of life's game to them.
- Want to contradict the truth.
- Want to tell only part of the truth.
- Want to keep a myth alive (e.g., Easter Bunny, Santa Claus, etc.).
- Believe the goal is not truth but persuasion.
- Are holding a "sacred" secret.
- Have advance information because of their position in the organization, but have to wait until a formal announcement is made.
- Don't believe anyone will be harmed if they withhold a bit of the truth.
- Believe that, in some situations, withholding the truth is an act of compassion.

Your listening and good basic communication skills can make a big difference in whether or not people tell you the truth. You can't afford to make a critical decision only to find out later that it was based on false or misleading information. It's important for you to be able to figure out whether you're being lied to, and whether there is something in your own behavior that might encourage others to lie to you. Recognizing the behaviors that signal when the whole story isn't being told and knowing what questions to ask, and when, can help you cut through deception and lying and have confidence in your communication.

Before we examine some of the cues that you might look and listen for, let's explore the behavior of lying. Anytime you develop a list of behaviors that distinguish liars from nonliars, you face two major problems. First, there are many types of lies (e.g., prepared or not, short answer or extended narrative, interrogated or not), and second, there are a variety of reasons for lying (e.g., to protect oneself; to protect someone else; to get out of an obligation, trust, or promise; to avoid conflict). In presenting the information below, we are *not* suggesting that you become an artful liar, but rather an artful listener who understands how lies are formed in the mind of the speaker.

- Effective liars consciously or unconsciously believe that practice makes perfect. When they're practicing, they don't lie about everything, but rather lie about little inconsequential things people wouldn't have any reason to believe they would lie about. These lies are beneath the radar screen, which make them an effective way to practice without being labeled a liar. For example, who's going to get suspicious if someone says that he had an omelet for breakfast when, in fact, he really had toast? This is the first step in practicing the art of lying—lying about the little things that don't raise any red flags.

• Effective liars make lies and facts sound the same. If their lies sound just like the truth, people won't know if they're lying or not. How do they do this? In practice, they think of something that's true and make it sound a lie. They practice sounding uncertain about saying it. Effective liars learn other people's patterns of listening. They know that, if you get used to hearing them say things that are true the same way they tell lies, when they actually tell a lie, it will be harder for you to separate the lie from the truth.

• Effective liars get their facts straight before they lie. They know the biggest risk in telling a lie is getting caught either contradicting themselves or saying something that obviously can't or didn't happen. They also realize that lying is often a "one and done" thing: Once they are labeled a liar, it will be hard to change that perception of them. Remember the story of the boy who cried "wolf" too often.

• Effective liars combine some truth with their lies. Outright lies are much easier to detect than lies that have an element of truth to them. Obviously, the more truth to a lie, the harder it is to detect what's true and what's not.

• Some of the most effective liars are those who manipulate the listener to do the lying for them. They imply lies. They do not put the actual lie into words, but imply that what they're saying is true. They lay the groundwork to lead you to believe what is true without actually saying it. They then have deniability if you ever discover what they said—or rather what you *thought* they said—was a lie. They can simply say that they never actually said that; you just misread what they were saying.

What are some of the signals that might alert you that someone is lying to you? Experts say that when people are lying, they may

- Avoid eye contact or shift their glance often.
- Stutter, pause, or clear their throat repeatedly.
- Change voice tone or volume.
- Offer multiple excuses for a situation.
- Stand in a defensive position.
- Redden slightly on the face or neck.
- Rub, stroke, or pull on their nose.
- Deflect attention from the issue.
- Appear uncomfortable.

So, in answer to the question, "How do you listen to someone who you feel or know is lying to you?" you listen strategically and with empathy, just as you do in every situation, to develop the understanding you need to respond effectively. The bottom line is this: Remember that not everybody with whom you come in contact always tells the truth at all times and in all situations.

Now, how many lies have you told today? Did you tell someone that his really ugly tie looks great? Did you tell your wife that those new jeans don't make her look fat? Lies, little white ones and gigantic ugly ones, are, unfortunately, a social reality. Before you tell lies to others, here are a few questions to ask yourself:

- Will anyone be harmed if I withhold a bit of the truth?
- Will this person change and grow from my honest feedback, or am I being unnecessarily blunt by giving an honest opinion that is hurtful?
- How would I feel if someone withheld the truth from me under the same circumstances?
- Is avoiding the truth in this particular situation an act of cowardice or of compassion?

Most of us lie to some degree, especially when faced with an alternative like hurting someone's feelings.

As an administrator in a school district, you often know district secrets (e.g., the closing of a building, the transfer of personnel, long-range plans under development, etc.). The ever-present grapevine and inevitable information leaks cause potentially affected people to ask you about what they heard. When that happens, you're placed in a position of being forced to say something like, "I haven't heard anything about that" or "I don't know anything about that." You know that you're lying, but you really don't have a choice in the matter; you know that if you respond by stating that you know about that, but you can't comment on it, it may have an adverse effect on your credibility with the people you supervise. Sometimes, withholding the truth or lying is a part of your job, albeit an unpleasant part.

INTERRUPTED LISTENING

Interruptions are one glitch in trying to be a good listener in the nonlinear culture of school administration. The information presented below is paraphrased from Dunklee (2000). Look at the two statements that follow and think about how difficult but critical it is to cultivate strategic listening skills when interruptions occur in your day-to-day management and leadership activities:

- Most administrative activities are short, fragmented, and verbal (Bogotch & Roy, 1997), and school leaders find themselves constantly involved in events that are initiated by interruptions.
- School leaders are apt to make the poorest decisions when they are interrupted early in the *listening* process or late in the *decision-making* process.

An interruption causes a predictable sequence of events, as the following scenario illustrates. Suppose you're in the middle of listening to a teacher, Betty, and suddenly you're interrupted by another teacher, Ted. In this scenario, you are the principal. Let's call you Richard.

Betty: Richard, I think that we should be looking at making some additional changes in our curricular strategies to more closely match the required skills necessary for our kids to pass the state-mandated standardized tests. I've thought about this, and I'd like to outline what I think. First, I suggest that we closely examine both our vertical and horizontal articulation before we embark on . . .

[Enter Ted]

Ted: Richard, Betty, I'm sorry to interrupt but—well, there's a leak in the ceiling in my room. . . .

Now, you've got two people, Betty and Ted, to accommodate at the same time and you don't want to short-change either of them. You've been interrupted while you've been actively listening to Betty to fully comprehend and build the factual foundation you need to address her concern. You now have Betty's unfinished narrative in your mind while you're receiving entirely different information and concerns from Ted.

Ted: And it's dripping on the new carpet!

You put Betty's case aside to hear what Ted has to say. Now, you quickly move into a phase of *progressive retrieval* (Gronn, 1983). In other words, Ted has exhausted his vocalization of the problem, and you've put Ted's needs foremost in your mind—at the expense of Betty's concerns. And now you're ready to make an informed and immediate decision to resolve Ted's concerns.

You: There's a bucket in the custodial closet, Ted. You go get it while I find a custodian to send to your room to help.

Clearly, Ted's dilemma requires careful listening, but not much more than a "bucket approach." A substantial number of school-based interruptions require more than just a bucket, however. They require considerate strategic listening to produce a positive outcome.

Once you contact a custodian as promised, you need to regenerate your conversation with Betty.

You: Sorry about that, Betty. Where were we?

Now, keeping the Betty and Ted scenario in mind, let's dissect what's happening. An incident occurred. Betty proceeded to give you the information you need to understand her issues. In a perfect world, Betty would have been able to complete her presentation to you without interruption. You, then, would be able to think through the decision-making process and arrive at some satisfactory conclusion, also without interruption.

However, Ted interrupted your conversation with Betty. You dealt with the interruption and then returned to Betty. If Betty had presented almost all of her concerns to you before the interruption, and if you believe that you were able to retain those concerns, then you and Betty can pick up from where she left off. If not, you and Betty must restart the speaking and listening process from the beginning.

It's interesting to note that the most important points that Betty wants you to hear will probably be stated, up front, during the beginning of the conversation. If you're interrupted before the main points have been made, you probably should restart the conversation. If you're interrupted closer to the middle of Betty's presentation, you can assume, with caution, that points made later in the conversation will be repetitions of earlier ideas. The timing of the interruption determines how much backtracking you need to do before you can move the conversation along. You had listened to Betty's declaratory sentence, and you recall that she was starting to list specific suggestions. You may be able to continue from this point without loss of information.

When you return to Betty to hear the rest of what she has to say, you again become a strategic listener. Now, you can measure her salient points, weigh her suggestions and potential outcomes, picture your potential decision within the overall culture with which you're working, and make your decision.

You: Betty, let's do it! I like your suggestions. Let me know what you need from me. Betty, is that . . . is that water I see trickling around the corner? I had better go and check on Ted.

A subunit of listening strategically through interruptions is keeping your priorities straight when emotions are involved. Equally important in listening for information gathering is attending to the speaker's collateral or resultant emotional level. Often, even as the immediate physical facts are presented (Betty's curricular suggestions and Ted's water problem), the speaker's emotional involvement intensifies. If you focus only on gathering the facts of an incident, you may overlook any emotional baggage the speaker is carrying into the description of the incident or problem. For example, let's add some words to Ted's communication. First, Ted told you in very few words, "There's a leak in the ceiling in my room—and it's dripping on the new carpet!" You heard "leak," "ceiling," Ted's "room," and perhaps "new carpet." That's about all you needed to hear in this situation to make your decision.

Now, consider if Ted had added such statements as, "My whole day is ruined!" "It's a conspiracy!" "I think someone is out to ruin my reputation as a teacher!" "Some of the water, or whatever it is, splashed on me and now I'm feeling feverish!" Ridiculous, you say? Not so. You're dealing with human emotions or perceptions, not just cold, hard physical facts. What you don't know is what might have happened to Ted prior to the immediate incident. That morning, he may have had problems at home with his wife or car trouble on the way to school. After arriving at school, Ted may have had a problem with a coworker or a student. While you're collecting physical facts about the incident, it's important that you also sense the speaker's tone of voice, body language, and other clues the speaker presents to you spontaneously coupled with the facts.

Strategic listening is concerned not only with the physical problem at hand, but also with the emotional dilemma it may be causing the speaker. In Ted's case, a bucket and a custodian may satisfy the physical situation, but if an elevated emotional state has been added to the paradigm, you may well have to tell Betty that you'll continue your conversation with her later. Attending to Ted's emotional stability is your new and immediate priority.

To fully understand what a speaker is trying to communicate, you have to assume that the speaker is expressing his or her true feelings and sentiments, and that the words alone are not the complete message. To understand another's feelings and sentiments, you need to find the context for them by looking for referents to the speaker's words in life events and social situations to understand the full meaning of those words.

WORKING WITH ASL AIDES TO ENSURE CORRECT MESSAGE DELIVERY

All special children and parents need particular attention in the learning, teaching, and administrative environment of the school, and our communication must meet their particular listening needs. Although we'd like to address this issue in depth, it really constitutes another entire book. Still, we want to provide some thoughts about working with American Sign Language (ASL) aides (interpreters) to the hearing impaired and deaf.

When working with interpreters for the hearing impaired or deaf, your interest is in ensuring that they are accurately interpreting the words, inflection, and emotional quality you are communicating in your words, tone of voice, and paralanguage. To test an interpreter's comprehensive delivery of your message, you might ask them the following questions:

- How did you feel while recreating my presentation?
- Do you think that your inflection mirrored mine?
- Do you believe, from your point of view, that all audience members, both hearing and nonhearing, have the same understanding of my message?

Unfortunately, the hearing impaired regularly encounter people who do not use their language (ASL), and they often depend on body language and facial expressions to understand the environment and the message. Because nonverbal information is the hearing impaired's primary source of information, you need to remind interpreters to make sure that they accurately communicate the intended message by exhibiting the appropriate nonverbal (facial and body) language as well as signing your words. For example, a sense of insecurity of the part of the signer (Did I sign that correctly?) can turn your straightforward statement into a question for the nonhearing listener. To convey your complete message, the interpreter has to accurately observe the nonverbal information you are presenting and convert that information into a visual format for the nonhearing recipient.

Whether you consider yourself to be a dynamic or just an average speaker, you need to seek out a dynamic signer. Your message, no matter what your presentation style, needs to be "heard equally" by all. Hearing impaired and deaf people, in general, have highly experienced eyes and normally receive the signer's body language first and then the speaker's words. You're always communicating visual information, and it is the job of the interpreter to be aware of what is communicated and to convey, as accurately as possible, the paralinguistic information, as well as the verbal message.

5 Listening to Your Constituencies and Managing Your Allegiance

It is the province of knowledge to speak. And it is the privilege of wisdom to listen.

—Oliver Wendell Holmes

Every school is alive with distinct, stimulating, and often unpredictable events each day. Morris, Crowson, Porter-Gehrie, and Hurwitz (1984) noted that school leaders live in a world they describe as "fluid." In a typical school, they found that

- Actors on the political stage are constantly changing, contradictions abound, and solutions to problems often do not last.
- One group of parents may oppose another.
- Factions may develop among the school staff, and some of these will ally with outside groups.
- The controls exercised by the organizational hierarchy may change as chief officers come and go.

- The decisions of federal bureaucrats or the judiciary, the whims of the state legislatures, and the initiatives of local politicians may alter the rules of the managerial game.
- The pressures from above that force a change in policy may be met by an equally powerful counterforce from staff members and parents below. To bow to one is to alienate the other; to compromise by bending a rule may alienate both.

As a school leader, your professional life balances precariously in a tug-of-war between competing interests and multiple constituencies. To be effective, you need to develop both a high tolerance for ambiguity and refined listening skills. You also need to function effectively when your power is limited and the direction of the educational system is sometimes unclear. Your ability to lead, and to succeed, generally hinges on your ability to listen to, engage with, and integrate special interests and multiple constituencies, effectively blending them into a working unit.

School and school district leadership is more complicated, ambiguous, and behind-the-scenes than most people imagine. Walsh (1998) noted,

There's politics around every corner. We'll make decisions at the school, but if a certain group of parents don't like them, all of a sudden there's a barrage of letters and phone calls and a decision floats down from above contrary to everything that was worked out at the school level. Today a school principal has to be more "the principal politician" than what he or she was intended to be—"the principal teacher," based on the British concept of the headmaster. Constantly dodging bullets and having to placate this and that individual or group, a principal has less time to be an instructional leader. (p. C5)

As a school leader, you have to listen and respond to the demands of an array of masters. Your first responsibility is to manage the unpredictability of three key areas of the school community: student discipline and control, teacher and staff performance, and parent and community involvement. In addition, you have to listen to, understand, and respond to the workings of central administration and individual Board of Education members. Further, you have to manage both stabilization and school improvement initiatives to harmoniously unite multiple constituencies, in spite of the fact that a high degree of tension frequently exists between such initiatives. Too much stabilization can deaden the enterprise; too many enhancements can be disorienting, counterproductive, and sometimes risky.

There are other constituencies to whom you must listen and answer as well. These include local business owners, neighborhood churches, local civic groups and clubs, and so forth. Moreover, there is a body politic that affects and influences education decision making, even though it has no legal authority to do so. It includes (and the list here is far from complete) such groups as

- The National Education Association and other similar associations/unions
- Professional associations that represent the various subjects taught in schools
- Trade publications
- Legal action groups, such as the NAACP and the American Civil Liberties Union, that influence education policy by promoting or assisting in key litigation
- Parent groups, such as the PTA, that are active lobbyists for their education concerns
- Agencies and companies, such as the Educational Testing Service, that prepare standardized tests and that, by virtue of the widespread use of these standardized tests, monitor and report the so-called conditions of our districts by state and nationwide

In one of the earliest sociological explanations of life in schools, Waller (1965) noted that the social world of the local school is a "tangled web of interrelationships" between human beings "who have much in common but are also in conflict" (p. 2). Teachers, administrators, students, and parents relate to one another in the confined setting of the school quite often as antagonistic forces existing in a state of perilous equilibrium. It's your job to effectively manage the school's environment to ensure a controlled setting for teaching and learning and to provide leadership for students, faculty, and staff, empowering them to focus on excellence in their individual roles.

LISTENING STRATEGICALLY TO AND INTERACTING WITH YOUR MULTIPLE CONSTITUENCIES

A number of constituencies or subcultures impact your day-to-day activities and continually test your ability to lead. As a school leader, it's your responsibility to meld these disparate interests into a working unit, attending simultaneously to both institutional and individual needs. You have to make yourself available, approachable, and able to listen thoughtfully to others and to convey the message that you are as concerned about them as the situation being addressed. The feedback you give needs to communicate your appreciation of the content and meaning of both the message and their feelings.

In our experience, thinking about communication as a people process rather than a language process is a strategy that enables us to receive and transmit both oral and written messages effectively. You may find the following techniques useful in listening strategically to your constituencies:

- When beginning a conversation with others, keep in mind that they are the consumers for your ideas. Their decisions about whether to buy in will greatly influence your results.

- Begin listening with a neutral, open mind so you can focus on what the speaker is saying.

- Pay attention to the logical content of what the speakers say, but be attentive to how they say it to discover their true feelings about the subject. When you listen for emotions as well as words, you gain a deeper understanding of how and why the subject is important to the speaker.

- Make a point of responding to speakers in a way that verifies that you are taking them seriously. Always demonstrate respect for the speaker's point of view.

Now, let's take a closer look at the constituencies that have the most direct impact on your work.

Students

Your students are required by law to attend school, and the prescribed curriculum may not be relevant to their immediate interests. Although many students truly enjoy school, there is often strong peer pressure to resist the education process. Because their primary interest is in fitting into, and being accepted by, the society of their peers, they are frequently hesitant to communicate openly with you. In addition, young people exist in their own world and speak their own language. If you're not tuned in to their world, you may misunderstand or misinterpret what they're saying.

In a recent *Washington Post* article describing a cultural competence program sponsored by the University of Maryland, Schulte (2004) noted that educators need special communication and connecting skills when working with urban students.

An educator stated as he explained his problems in communicating with his inner-city students.

Their [students'] reality was not my reality, The idea is that until urban educators 'get' their students—their distinct cultures, their languages, their home lives, their perceptions of the world and their place in it . . . urban educators will never effectively reach these students. Many educators are scared of their students. All they know about their students' culture is what they see on TV (p. B1).

One educator interviewed by Schulte (2004) explained how he attempts to maintain cultural competence. The educator noted that he

doesn't have to like the music his students listen to, but he does need to know about it. He does need to make sure that the way his classroom looks and the materials he chooses include people stories that his students can relate to. As long as you listen the educator concludes you can build relationships no matter what your background is (p. B1).

As you well know, suburban and rural students have different but equally distinct cultures that can also challenge your ability to communicate effectively with them.

To listen strategically to students, you need to

- Understand basic human growth and development theories.
- Keep up with current elementary, adolescent, and young adult trends, fads, movies, TV shows, and ways of thinking.
- Be aware of their relationships with other students, family, and others.
- Respond to their physical, emotional, and general security needs.
- Listen carefully to teenagers and explore what they are thinking and how they came to their conclusions.
- Remember that younger children are just learning words and are constantly searching for the right ones. That's why you hear the "um, um, um" before they say something. Be patient.
- Recognize that students like to give advice and share opinions if they feel respected. Listening to them can help you see the school through their eyes and gain valuable insights.
- Eliminate distractions in the environment.
- Be aware that children of all ages can be strongly affected by the tone of your voice and your facial and body expressions, and manage your tone and gestures accordingly.

Teachers

The majority of teachers are committed to their profession and to the welfare of their students. They tend to be equally interested in both an orderly working and teaching environment and their own well being (think evaluation), and they want you to listen to every word they say. Teachers are a special breed. In spite of the importance of their jobs, they comprise one of the most insecure groups of workers in today's society.

This insecurity, we believe, is caused by a number of environmental elements. First, teacher isolation, one of the most obvious realities of teachers' professional lives, promotes insecurity and inhibits both growth and the confidence that they are doing a good job. Second, semester after semester, year after year, teachers must work with children and young adults who demonstrate increasingly varied levels of learning abilities. Third, teachers often consider the school their home away from home: They develop deep ownership in their rooms, and as every principal who has moved teachers from one room to another knows, have strong attachments to their desks, chairs, blackboards, bulletin boards, and so on.

Your teachers expect you to provide stability and leadership, not just in the school setting, but in their personal lives as well. In the school setting, they look to you for guidance and direction, instructional and disciplinary strategies, supplies and equipment, room décor, and much more. What they most want from you is recognition of their efforts and respect for their expertise. With regard to their personal lives, you've probably, as we have, helped teachers deal with such difficulties as the deaths of parents or children, divorces, affairs, financial problems, and other dilemmas.

In spite of—or possibly due to—their commitment to education, teachers frequently perceive administrators as the enemy. This is especially true where teacher unions are strong. Your ability to listen effectively, often more so than your actions, is the key to building an energetic and competent faculty.

When working with teachers, the key listening skill is empathy. You demonstrate empathy by

- Being other-directed, rather than projecting your own feelings and ideas onto those being shared with you.
- Being non-defensive and open to the speaker's thoughts and concerns.
- Recognizing that the other person's perspective and experience may well be quite different from your own.
- Listening primarily as a receiver, not as a critic, with a desire to understand the speaker in order to achieve mutual agreement or provide guidance in problem solving.

Support and Staff Personnel

Custodians, Secretaries, and Clerks

Secretaries, clerks, and custodians may be more concerned with working conditions and job security than in creating an orderly teaching and learning environment. Listening to these staff members can be problematic. For example, this group often exaggerates problems and can easily forget that students, parents, and teachers—not routine tasks—are their first priority. We see this group as the "listen, support, and praise" group. Without assistance from you, they may place undue emphasis on trivial events. They can become bogged down by two obvious challenges that characterize and can impede their work: dealing with multiple tasks and communicating with varied audiences.

A principal we know discovered that there was an entire hidden culture in her school she hadn't even suspected. She had a troublesome night custodial supervisor who complained several times that the day custodian was using his, the night man's, cleaning supplies. The principal could have headed off a human resources issue if she had understood the district's custodial culture. It seems that the night custodians are trained to mix solutions and get all of their equipment ready for the next night's shift at the end of the current shift—and it's a major breach of custodial etiquette for someone else to use their tools or supplies. Once the employee relations person in human resources explained the situation to the principal, she resolved to listen more closely to what her staff told her in the future.

Custodians can be very supportive of an orderly teaching and learning environment when your praise or constructive criticism is linked back to the school mission. For example, imagine the potential result when you respond to custodial complaints by saying, "Your crew's hard work is really making the school a great place for kids to feel comfortable and safe enough to learn," or, "I know the district doesn't expect you to take such good care of the throw rugs the teachers bring in on their own, but they really appreciate the fact that you do. Some afternoon, take a look at the kids working on those nice clean rugs." Listening to your custodians and helping them reframe their concerns based on student learning can produce the desired results.

The concerns of the office staff can be reframed as well. They are often the heartbeat of the building, and teachers, parents, and students are always taking their pulses. Secretaries and clerks who feel listened to are more apt to appreciate the important role they play as members of your school's instructional and public relations teams.

Counselors

Counselors work with students, parents, and, occasionally, teachers to resolve individual problems ranging from personal and family concerns to schedules and difficult school relationships. Because of the nature of their job responsibilities, counselors frequently work in isolation from your office. As a result, they can become detached from current and planned administrative prerogatives and the day-to-day concerns of faculty and staff. Effective principals schedule time to share information and direction with counselors to keep them involved in the overall school program. They recognize that counselors do their best work when they are not bogged down with administrative chores. To reinforce the idea that your counselors are not administrators, when discussing policy or procedural changes with them, you need to define their role as strictly advisory, not determinative. In general, your interactions with your counselors should be open-ended with both you and the counselors sharing equally in listening and talking.

In our experience, counselor burnout is frequently a potential problem. You need to listen carefully to identify any signs of stress revealed by a counselor's words or body language and intercede to resolve some of the counselor's frustrations as warranted. You also should listen for signs of a counselor's over-involvement in a particular situation on which he or she might be working. This is a matter of risk management for principals, and a potentially serious safety issue for counselors.

Program Coordinators and Department Heads

School-based program coordinators or department heads provide effective means for secondary principals to keep tabs on the workings of the multiple programs inherent in a vibrant high school. Similarly, elementary principals frequently find that primary and intermediate school program coordinators can take significant time-management pressures away from their offices.

Effective elementary principals recognize the importance of designated teachers as primary and intermediate program heads. Strong teachers in these positions can be extremely helpful in developing the master schedule, placing itinerant teachers, setting the ever-present recess schedule and assigning appropriate supervision, helping with textbook selection and ordering, stocking the supply closet, and more. They can also provide you, on an informal basis, with insights on how to work with new teachers or those who may be in need of improvement. When they speak to you, listen carefully, because what they say is important to the smooth running of your elementary school. If you develop a habit of listening, your lead teachers can help you pinpoint the needs of their colleagues, giving you the opportunity to help them contact district specialists who can help with staff development and instructional issues.

At the secondary school level, we can't overemphasize the importance of effective department chairs. As a middle or high school principal, no matter how "renaissance" you think you are, you can't be an expert in all the various academic and nonacademic disciplines included in a typical secondary school curriculum. Effective department heads can manage and, if you're lucky, lead faculty toward successful completion of your goals and aspirations for the academic units. We think of this group of faculty leaders as our "listen to and learn" group. Listening strategically to this group can give you informal insights into your faculty's thoughts and needs. You can successfully launch trial balloons through your department heads and receive insightful feedback and advance information you can use to develop strategies for change.

In recent years, at the high school and, in some areas, the middle school level, we have seen the responsibilities of the typical athletic coordinator position expanded to include scheduling and oversight of all extracurricular activities. Although replacing the athletic coordinator with an activity coordinator has helped to resolve many problems, the expanded title may have created a monster job loaded with stress. As a secondary school leader, you need to listen strategically to your activity coordinator, provide the tools necessary to keep him or her on track, and clearly communicate that you consider him or her a highly valuable member of the school's overall administrative team. Although the activity coordinator is generally not part of the policy-making team, this individual can be an effective advisor to your office. Here, again, you need to listen for signs of potential burnout.

Librarians and Media Specialists

Librarians or media specialists, like counselors, work with a multitude of students, teachers, and parents on a diverse variety of projects and issues. They work to solve individual reading issues, facilitate research assignments or interests, and frequently develop positive mentoring relationships with students as well. Like counselors, because of the nature of their job responsibilities, they frequently work in isolation from your office. They, too, can be distanced from administrative plans and policies and the day-to-day concerns of faculty and staff. Occasional informal meetings with your librarians can help you keep them in the mainstream of the instructional program. It also allows you to hear what problems or concerns they might be experiencing in their particular jobs and what you can do to assist. Given your ear, they frequently can identify instructional needs.

Specialist Teachers

Function-focused teachers may be the most often cursed and equally beloved group of people in your school. These specialists in the arts and athletics typically strive for perfection in end results and often tweak rules, regulations, policies, and procedures in the process. Although they frequently enable students to experience success, they can be both a pain in your neck and a sweet-smelling flower in your lapel.

Even though these creative and highly charged but effective individuals are often 100% function-focused, they often make excellent informal mentors to troubled students. Your goal may be to direct their attention to their roles as part of the instructional team and encourage them to focus on process as well as products. But don't overlook the fact that they can share valuable insights with you if you can slow them down long enough to listen. Because perfection is their goal, in spite of their surface enthusiasm, they may need your empathy and understanding, regardless of the hassles you may suffer as a result of their antics.

Assistant Principals

Assistant principals usually don't make administrative or policy decisions. Instead, they are responsible for implementing decisions made by you or the administrative team as a whole. Their myriad responsibilities are subject to your immediate and diverse needs. Because their primary interest is usually to achieve results that will encourage you to recommend a continuing contract or promotion, when you interact with your assistant principals, they listen carefully to every word you say. You need to listen strategically to them to provide them with the guidance, support, and recognition they seek on a daily basis. By listening strategically in your interactions with your assistant principals, you can help them to develop their leadership skills by discussing such important issues as

- Strategies to help with decision making.
- Ideas to develop communications.
- Ways to build relationships with constituencies.
- The reality that change takes time.
- The fact that the principal's job is often reactive rather than proactive.

- The basics of crisis management and litigation avoidance.
- Ways to delegate tasks and tips on scheduling, organization, and time management.
- Ways to develop and maintain a strong network of colleagues.
- Insider information regarding daily or standard operating procedures not found in manuals or regulations.
- Contract interpretation.
- The need to be assertive in actions and confident in decisions.
- Ways to enjoy and rise above the challenges of the job.

Central Office Administrators

Central office administrators include two distinct subgroups: line administrators and staff administrators. Line administrators include the superintendent, associate and assistant superintendents, and other executives who report directly to the superintendent. Their primary responsibilities are to direct, control, monitor, and evaluate employee performance and budget management and to designate preferred outcomes for district-wide programs. They exercise top-down authority in their roles as planners, examiners, and evaluators; establish and maintain vertical lines of communication; and develop written policies, procedures, rules, and regulations that set standards and guide administrative actions. To address problems that arise from changing conditions, they may add supervisory and administrative staff positions to the hierarchy of the organization. They are also the key evaluators of your work and interpret your successes or failures to the board of education.

Staff administrators typically report to an assistant superintendent, and their primary responsibilities are to coordinate budgets, personnel, or programs. As school districts expand in size (population, programs, etc.), staff positions (such as districtwide chairpersons, directors, specialists, directors of districtwide activities, coordinators of special programs, etc.) tend to multiply. The larger the district, the more complex the bureaucracy becomes.

Both line and staff administrators tend to see themselves as being on the "front line," whereas principals see themselves as being on the "firing line," and teachers see themselves as being on both the "front" and the "firing" lines. Without effective management by line administrators, disagreements can develop between staff administrators and building principals as to who has final authority in determining what is right for individual schools.

Most school leaders realize that they can listen passively and uncritically or actively and critically. Listening to line and staff administrators, for the most part, requires your best active and critical listening skills.

You've probably experienced, as we have, that it's not always easy to understand what line and staff administrators say or mean, and it can be difficult to integrate their thinking into your own. You have to translate the words of line and staff administrators into ideas that make sense to you—interpret them through the filters of your experiences and what you know.

Understanding what central office administrators expect of you is clearly critical to your professional well being, and a good way to clarify what these administrators are saying is to ask questions. Because you never want your questions to present a direct challenge to the speaker's words or thoughts, an effective strategy is to ask for help in understanding. Ask, for example, "I'm not sure I understand you when you say. . . . Could you explain that further?" "Could you give me an example or illustration of what you see?" "Would you also say that . . .?" "Let me see if I understand you. What you are saying is this. . . . Is that right?" Strategic listening will help you identify the administrator's rationale or hidden agenda and what it may mean for your school.

Board of Education and the Local Community

Board of Education members are elected or selected by the community at large and are the legal authority for the community's public schools. The constituencies they represent expect allegiance to certain values and enforcement of constitutional safeguards. The values of the community as a whole—freedom of speech, tolerance of ethnic and religious differences, equal treatment, and the right to learn—should take precedence over local special interests. We say "should" simply because we know that, regardless of how hard a district works at effective Board of Education development, individual board member preferences and agendas often impede the board's work as a team.

School boards frequently comprise, as does your community at large, both informed and uninformed supporters or critics. We hope that your interactions with school board members are infrequent and that your district's superintendent has developed sufficient rapport with board members that they seek answers at that level, not through you.

The local community, like your Board of Education, voices parents' aspirations for their children and the neighborhood's interest in maintaining good schools, qualified teachers, and a livable environment. Educators maintain a tradition of professional autonomy and standards, and we assume that you share the teachers' view of the importance of instruction and the value of independence. However, your community, both its informed and uninformed members, can make or break your job as a school leader.

When dealing with critical school board members or other members of the community, you may find it effective to

- Keep the conversation centered on your particular school or situation, rather than allowing the conversation to become or involve a districtwide issue.
- Open the conversation or interaction in a way that elicits open-mindedness.
- Articulate your goals.
- Diagnose the other person's needs and problems by listening strategically and asking probing questions.
- Demonstrate respect for others' views and, at the same time, obtain respect for your own views.
- Raise the conversation up the intellectual and emotional ladder in a way that the other person is willing and able to follow all the way to the buy-in.

LISTENING TO ALL OF YOUR CONSTITUENCIES

When listening to your constituencies, you need to recognize that meaning is not in the words of the speakers, but rather in your—the receiver's—mind. Meaning is not transmitted; you give the message meaning based on your knowledge, experience, values, and prior observations. Because of differences in our backgrounds, words hold different meanings for different people, causing problems in semantics. Considering this, you should respond using words that are familiar to the speaker.

When listening to constituent concerns, pay close attention to the speaker's body language and use your skills as an interpreter of nonverbal cues to begin to frame your potential response. You have plenty of thinking time while you listen, because you can process an average of 500 words per minute while most people speak at about 125 words per minute. A deliberate speaker uses only a fraction of your thought capacity. Even as you maintain eye contact, observe and interpret the speaker's nonverbal signals, formulate questions to ask at appropriate moments to verify the accuracy of your understanding, and provide verbal and nonverbal feedback, you still have plenty of time to

- Outline the speaker's message.
- Identify the speaker's purpose and determine how the speaker's points support that purpose.
- Organize your listening by mentally summarizing the previous points and identifying the main points with key words or phrases.

- Evaluate the soundness of the speaker's logic.
- Verify and integrate information presented with your past knowledge and experience.
- Prepare to paraphrase the speaker's presentation and plan how you will respond.

MANAGING YOUR ALLEGIANCE

The fundamental questions—*To whom does the school leader owe his or her greatest loyalty? To whom does a school leader listen?*—continue to evade a simple answer. Many researchers have asked basically the same questions: Which of your multiple constituencies is your *primary* reference group when each group has a legitimate claim on your attention? How do you resolve this issue? Although many researchers have described the problem, none has developed a definitive answer.

One thing we've learned is that effective school leaders see and understand the ambiguities inherent in the school and school district environment. They listen to and balance the needs and desires of all the groups they serve with, for, and under. They balance their allegiance or loyalties in such a way that no group feels unimportant, un-listened to, or left out. Donaldson (1991) notes that

> more than anything else, the principal needs to learn how to keep the school functioning while he [*sic*] learns how he [*sic*] can move the many stakeholders [constituencies] in the school towards complementary visions of success. The job is never finished and the principal is never completely successful; but somehow the principal must do the equivalent of adjusting the engine of a powerful racing car while it is circling the track at 200 miles per hour. He [*sic*] dare not over-adjust, and the car must be kept on course. (p. 40)

As an effective school leader, you've learned how to routinize situations as rapidly as possible. Some theorists call this routinization *situational management*. Others point out that rather than discrete goal attainment, effective leaders practice *pattern rationality*. No matter what theoretical label you attach to the nonlinear events that make up the bulk of your work environment, successful practice requires the kind of strategic listening and quick thinking that enables you to constantly test what is happening against what you know. To be effective, you have to listen, think, practice, and act in linear ways, regardless of the nonlinear situations surrounding you.

The best overall school leaders continually read their audiences and use that ability to develop a constituent following. In the simplest of words, effective principals listen up front. They diagnose people's inclinations and the logic of their thoughts, needs, and wants. They find out precisely what it will take to provide leadership, contribute to teamwork, offer assistance, solve problems, or advance opportunities. Then, they act decisively on what they've heard and learned.

Strategic listening is a subtle but highly pragmatic skill that can provide you with the following:

- A clear informed vision of what you want your school or district to become
- An effective translation of this vision into clear goals and expectations for students and parents, faculty and staff, and administrators
- A school or district climate that supports the attainment of these goals and expectations

Think back along your own career path for a moment and we think you'll find, as we have, that those individuals who have influenced you the most were powerful listeners. Whether instinctively or through practice, they developed the skill of empathy. This is how we listen to our constituencies and how we believe effective school leaders maintain their positions as community leaders.

6 Strategic Listening to Build Trust

Courage is what it takes to stand up and speak; courage is also what it takes to sit down and listen.

—Winston S. Churchill

LISTENING TO SPAN BOUNDARIES

In the previous chapter, we examined the various constituencies you need to listen to and interact with effectively. It's your role as a leader, a problem solver, and a decision maker to act as a boundary spanner among the multiple constituencies in your school and district. Many problems in the education enterprise have their bases in misunderstandings. Generally, people assume that everyone has had the same experiences in life and that words have the same meaning for everyone. This is seldom true. You must listen actively to recognize both the differences and the similarities among your multiple constituencies.

As an effective leader, you have to listen for shared meaning among the participants of any conversation. The primary function of speech is to communicate ideas and feelings to others and to position people in relationship to one another. Meanings depend on the situation and the people in the situation. Shared meaning is not easy to achieve, because the subject is being discussed based on multiple sets of experiences. Arriving at shared meaning enables the participants in the conversation to share a window on a common reality. When you successfully hear and clarify the interrelationships among all the perceptions, the window opens—and the common reality becomes visible.

In listening to groups, you have to actively gather clues and filter information about organizational culture by watching to see whose presence is necessary for the group to function well, how decisions are made, how people are rewarded, and what priorities repeatedly get their attention. Doing so will allow you to focus your listening more directly toward individuals in the group to achieve the shared meaning and boundary spanning that significantly reduce the possibility of misunderstanding.

LEADERSHIP AND LISTENING: POSITIONING YOURSELF FOR TRUST

Before you can be an effective boundary spanner and provide the guidance and leadership your constituencies expect, they must trust you. Without trust, people will not share enough information to allow you to expand your understanding and help them provide solutions to problems or develop new possibilities for expediting change. Regardless of the knowledge, skills, competencies, and behavior you exhibit, effective leadership is possible only when other people (i.e., followers/speakers) trust you and grant you the power necessary to lead. People grant leader status to you based on their perceptions of who you are, what you stand for (your shared values and beliefs), and the degree to which you can be trusted to listen, speak, or act effectively on their behalf.

As a school leader, if you're not cautious, the current focus on *management* as the panacea for getting things done may hamper you in developing your listening skills. Unfortunately, most current and popular leadership theories, assessment methods, and state certification mandates are based on the *science* of management and administration, whereas effective leadership is an *art,* and strategic listening is the skill that promotes shared understanding.

There are identifiable competencies and behaviors that distinguish the effective listener and leader from the manager or administrator. Leaders seek to influence or change the behavior of other people; managers work with existing behaviors and organize and maintain routine work efforts. Leaders influence, whereas managers implement and administer. Leaders motivate and managers facilitate. The perceptions your constituents have of you are developed and aggregated over time as they observe and interpret your behaviors and actions in a variety of situations and circumstances. These perceptions of you and your ability to lead effectively are their aggregate impressions of your trustworthiness.

To be perceived as an effective leader, you have to listen strategically to identify, understand, respond to, and continuously manage the perceptions of others. In addition, you have to use this understanding to tailor the verbal and nonverbal messages you send to reinforce others' perception of your leadership. A powerful tool effective leaders use to maintain leadership over time is to assume different roles as changing circumstances dictate. These two closely related concepts, aggregate impression and role assumption, were identified by Dunklee (2000).

In his discussion of leadership competencies, abilities, and behaviors, Dunklee (2000) points out how important demeanor and deportment are to others' perceptions of your trustworthiness. Demeanor is the manner in which you present yourself, the way in which you outwardly manifest your personality or attitude and your communication style (especially your verbal style). Demeanor includes your characteristic posture and the customary ways in which you move and gesture when addressing others. Deportment is your actions, manners, behaviors, and conduct that was primarily molded by your upbringing and training. The amount of trust your constituents have in you is partially based on the extent to which you

- Exhibit personal and professional conduct, bearing, and appearance that conform to the conventions, proprieties, and mores of the enterprise and the greater community.
- Use words and gestures, exemplify attitudes, and act in ways that are consistent with a genuine respect for the rights and dignity of others.
- Model the desirable leadership qualities of integrity, self-respect, self-confidence, vision, patience, perseverance, and courage.
- Act in a consistent and ethical manner.

YOUR AGGREGATE IMPRESSION: BUILDING TRUST OVER TIME

The degree of trustworthiness your constituents recognize is based on their aggregate impression that what they say to you will be heard accurately and acted upon. The question now is, How do you provide your multiple constituencies with the kinds of impressions, over time, that will lead them to believe they'd like to follow you and share with you their concerns, ideas, or problems?

Given that the way people perceive you is likely to influence their interpretation of your behavior and the course of your future interactions and communications with them, understanding the perception process is important to the development of your leadership ability. Let's look at an overview of that process.

The Perception Process

General Impression

When we meet you for the first time, we begin to form a *general impression* almost immediately. Although such a general impression may be inaccurate, we develop a sense of your personality and traits and whether we like or dislike you. This is the starting point of our aggregate impression of you. For example, in our first meeting, our initial reactions are based on whatever fragmentary information is available. This information may be based on hearsay, reputation, or documented history, or may be limited to physical or social characteristics (e.g., you're tall, attractive, well dressed, well spoken, etc.).

Although our initial reactions may not possess a high degree of certainty, we develop general impressions of you with remarkable ease and speed. In addition, our initial reactions are often augmented by inferences concerning what else about you is likely to be true. These inferences are frequently based on stimuli such as those discussed above under demeanor and deportment, as well as on physical attractiveness, gender, race, age, and so forth. This evaluative bias, or *halo effect*, occurs normally in inference processes.

Primary Impression

If we meet or observe you only once, we may never develop an impression beyond the initial general one. However, when we expect to interact with you over time, we want as much information about you as possible. We immediately begin to augment our general impressions by making inferences about what else is likely to be true about you. These are called *primary impressions*. Whether such inferences are valid or invalid is irrelevant at this point in the process. Our inferences are "true" for us and will have an important bearing on our immediate perceptions of you.

As we get to know you better, we acquire more information (e.g., your style of interaction, free-time interests, aspirations, concerns, perceived strengths and weaknesses, or insecurities). With the acquisition of new information about you, we develop primary impressions that modify or elaborate our general perception of what you are like that can influence judgments we make about you.

Secondary Impression

When we work with you or encounter you on multiple occasions, over time we will continue to modify our perceptions based on our observations of your behavior or actions in different circumstances. To the extent that those actions confirm our expectations, they reinforce our primary impression. To the extent that your actions contradict our expectations, we add the new impressions to our initial ones. We gain a better, fuller picture of who you are and what we can expect from you in the future. These *secondary impressions* help us make decisions about whether we like you, are comfortable in your presence, and would like to get to know you even better.

Tertiary Impression

Our third-level impressions, *tertiary impressions,* are closely tied to our personal value systems and are key to our decision to trust, make a commitment to, or follow you. We form these tertiary impressions when we observe your behaviors toward others we care about or your actions in situations that are value-laden for us or in which we have a vested interest. To the extent that you share our value systems and act or behave in a manner of which we approve, our impressions of you are enhanced. To the extent that we are disappointed in your behavior or actions, our impressions of you become more negative.

Aggregate Impression

Through ongoing observations of you, we form, supplement, interpret, and categorize our impressions in different ways. In doing so, we develop an *aggregate impression* that influences all of our perceptions of and interactions with you. Each new piece of information we receive reinforces or modifies our aggregate impression. Our aggregate impression of you is, therefore, not fixed or rigid, but dynamic and subject to change over time. It can be very positive one day, negative the next, then positive again—depending on the behavior or actions we observe and the circumstances that surround them.

MANAGING OTHERS' PERCEPTIONS (AGGREGATE IMPRESSION) THROUGH ROLE ASSUMPTION

An important corollary to aggregate impression is that, if you are continuously aware of the perception development process, you can actively manage constituents' perceptions of your leadership abilities by behaving in ways that reinforce them. In reality, this means assuming different roles as circumstances dictate and being a good actor.

Effective leaders assume a different role each time they modify their behavior to achieve some desired goal, get someone to do something, persuade someone of something, or win trust or respect. In various circumstances in our diverse relationships, we all pursue our interests by behaving in certain ways. And, as is true in the theater, each role has its own appropriate behavior, speech, thought, and feelings, and each situation has its own character demands.

The different roles you assume should *never* be viewed by others as an act. Your constituents must continue to perceive your actions as genuine rather than manipulative. Just as the actor does, you can best express your listening skills by action—movement, gestures, tone of voice, and the creation and projection of character. We are not suggesting that you need to become a professional actor. However, the ability to assume different roles while maintaining integrity and to shift from role to role smoothly creates a powerful foundation for developing and maintaining an aggregate impression as a leader who is willing and able to be an effective listener.

7 An Insider's Look at Strategic Listening in Action

Too often we underestimate the power of a touch, a smile, a kind word, a listening ear, an honest compliment, or the smallest act of caring, all of which have the potential to turn a life around.

—Leo Buscaglia

One of the most important keys to your success as a school leader is the relationship you establish with your faculty and staff. At its most basic level, your relationship is based on the fact that you are the leader. On any given day, you are known as the boss, the supervisor, or any number of more or less flattering names. Whatever your faculty and staff call you when you're not around, you need to remember that you have a great deal of influence over them and their work.

In a school, as in any organization, there will be times when you won't get the real story of events from your faculty and staff. In most cases, they don't deliberately lie to you; they simply tend to distort information because they think they know what you want to hear. At best, they want to please you, and they don't want you to be angry with them. When information is passed to you in an altered state, it is called *upward distortion.*

Upward communication, discourse and information that flows from faculty and staff to you, is rarely candid or complete. Teachers, for example, tend to let you know what they want you to know and, if given the chance, will filter out information that reflects negatively on them. Their messages can be distorted due both to situational demands and to the difference between your power and the power they sense that they have. If your school climate is antagonistic or even hostile, teachers can resort to covert maneuvers in order to manipulate you. Experience teaches your faculty and staff that they can increase their influence with you if you see them as cooperative and supportive (Harris, 1993).

Partial or distorted information can keep you from getting a real picture of events and prevent you from solving problems as they arise (Shockley-Zalabak, 2002). As frustrating as this can be, you need to keep in mind that subtly reshaping the truth from one's own perspective is very human. If we're completely honest with ourselves, we can all recall times when we felt the need to put the best face on less than perfect situations.

School leaders generally spend one to two thirds of their workdays in communicating face-to-face with individuals who work for them. In her research on superior-subordinate relationships in the workplace, Shockley-Zalabak (2002) wrote that subordinates are more likely to be satisfied with their work and the way they are supervised if they feel that they communicate well with their supervisors. The strongest predictors of how satisfied people are with work and supervision are

- Their perception of their superior's ability to listen to them.
- How quickly their supervisor responds to their messages.
- If the superior is sensitive and understanding (Shockley-Zalabak, 2002).
- If they perceive that their supervisor is accessible to them (Harris, 1993).

Subordinates who report high-quality relationships with their supervisors are more likely to

- Engage in informal and friendly interactions with superiors.
- Conform to formal and informal requests by their supervisors.
- Attempt to clarify the expectations of their supervisors.
- Accept criticism from the supervisors (Shockley-Zalabak, 2002).

If we apply these findings to the relationships between school leaders and their subordinates, we can assume two things. First, subordinates who perceive that they have good two-way communication with their leaders enjoy being around them and thus share more information than teachers who do not perceive that they benefit from good two-way communication. Second, subordinates who have friendly relationships with their leaders may be motivated to work harder than usual to meet their superiors' expectations.

As a school leader, your long-term leadership effectiveness is firmly established in your ability to identify, understand, respond to, and continuously manage the perceptions of the people with whom you work. In order to do so, you must listen strategically to what your faculty and staff worry about, what motivates them, and what frustrates them. The benefits of your effective leadership will be passed on to your students.

In this era of accountability, effective school leaders are essential for student success. Dunklee (2000) noted the following regarding effective leaders:

- Effective leaders solve problems and make decisions.
- Effective leaders communicate.
- Effective leaders demonstrate sensitivity.

In order to effectively solve problems and make decisions, you need to obtain the most accurate information available and include appropriate individuals in the decision-making process. Only then can you assess the consequences that the decision will have on the community. You're more apt to acquire the best and most accurate information when you constantly listen to understand.

To communicate well, you have to determine what needs to be heard and then send the needed messages. You discreetly monitor gossip and small talk in order to take action when needed. You sense the anxieties and needs of others and respond to those emotions effectively and gracefully. You understand that individuals bring diverse backgrounds, experiences, and perceptions to the workplace. You observe, hear, absorb, and interpret verbal and nonverbal messages in order to read between the lines and to understand.

From our personal experience, we know that effective leaders are compassionate. Teachers work hard in a sometimes lonely and always demanding profession, and we understand that even the most gifted teachers need positive attention and well-earned praise. Having a good laugh with a teacher or staff member is always time well spent. We recognize that each teacher and staff member is a human being with a personal life that colors his or her perspective at work. We know this by listening strategically.

WHAT RESEARCH DEMONSTRATES ABOUT STRATEGIC LISTENING

Tate (2002) conducted a study to determine the degree to which principals who use and promote best practice and have good relationships with their staffs employ strategic listening strategies. The study involved numerous interviews with effective principals and some of their teachers. Although the principals with whom she talked had very different personalities and leadership styles, Tate found that nearly all of them use strategic listening skills as a part of their approach to leadership.

Excerpts from Tate's (2002) conversations with five of the principals studied and with selected teachers who worked for those principals are included in the Resources section at the end of this chapter. What follows is an overview of what her study revealed about effective principals and their use of strategic listening.

Every principal interviewed sincerely believed that he or she listened well. Each mentioned simple listening skills that included such techniques as using direct eye contact, using good body language, and asking probing questions. However, they also discussed strategic listening behaviors that were more than simply hearing words. Some of those behaviors included

- Sitting in on meetings with teachers.
- Walking around in the building to see what is going on.
- Observing teachers as they interact with colleagues and students.
- Being aware of teachers' needs and what is important to them.

According to the principals interviewed, listening is gathering information to help them better understand their teachers and what was going on in their schools. In their own words, principals discussed how they needed to stand back and observe or sit back and listen without talking. They spoke of listening to teachers and the messages between the lines. As they did listen, they interpreted the utterances, body language, and physical manifestations of teachers with whom they interacted to discover a greater meaning than could be conveyed simply in words.

The principals all made a point of saying that they were accessible to their staffs. Their respective teachers liked the idea of an open-door policy.

They were pleased to have access to their principals, and they made a point of saying so.

As mentioned earlier, the major characteristics people want in their leaders is a sense of purpose, a sense of trust, optimism, and the ability to obtain results (Bennis, 1997). Therefore, it is crucial for you, as a school leader, to listen carefully to your faculty and staff in order to hear between the lines of the conversations with which you deal every day. When you listen strategically, you will be better able to make sense of the endless demands placed on you.

The principals interviewed by Tate (2002) envisioned themselves as understanding and often compassionate school leaders. The teachers interviewed frequently noted the importance of feeling that they had a personal connection with their principals. Furthermore, they emphasized how important it is for them to have pleasant, informal working relationships with their principals. Not a single principal mentioned having fun or joking around with their respective teachers to build personal connections with them and to build trust, but the teachers said differently. They seemed almost proud that they had the kind of professional friendship with their respective principals that allowed them to joke around and enjoy a moment or two of good-natured humor. To Tate (2002), statements like those that follow demonstrated an aura of trust:

- "My principal is fun to be with. She does things like walking with us to raise money for cancer research, and she enthusiastically supports every school function and project."
- "When things get a little boring at inservices, we can joke around with each other."
- "Somehow we just click when we're around each other. We have a really good time sitting together when we get invited to teachers' baby showers or wedding receptions."
- "His sense of humor is great! It's natural and doesn't poke fun at anybody. He can really liven things up."
- "Sometimes we 'cut up' in the office when the kids aren't around."

Building Community

In Tate's (2002) study, it was very important to the teachers interviewed that their principals gave them their full attention when they listened. Teachers said that when their principals listened to them, their words seemed more valuable or meaningful. All of the principals, to one degree or another, demonstrated strategic listening skills that seemed to help them better understand what motivated their teachers.

Strategic listening builds a sense of community between principals and their faculties and staffs. Every principal interviewed described the ways in which he or she built the trust that is the foundation of community. Several principals said they never broke confidences. Another thought that it was important to accept the faults of his teachers, just as he hoped they would accept his own faults. Two principals said they made a point of letting their teachers know they genuinely cared about them. One stated that he had a personal theory that caring and trust are intertwined.

In addition to the positive values expressed about building a community based on trust, most principals solicited the opinions of their teachers in decision making. Those principals seemed to appreciate and look forward to collaborating with their teachers. In addition, four of the principals mentioned that they delegated responsibilities to teachers and encouraged them to participate in staff development activities and try new ideas. As one said, "Give them wings and they fly."

The teachers indirectly expressed their trust in their principals by describing their informal professional relationships with them. They liked having principals who were accessible to them and appreciated opportunities to give their opinions about things that affected the school. They liked the idea that they could share concerns with the principal. It was important to the teachers that their respective principals demonstrate that they cared about faculty and staff. One teacher seemed to find it meaningful that his principal made it clear the teachers' families had priority over anything associated with school. A special education teacher spoke softly as she described her principal's reaction when she told her that her father was dying. "What do you want me to do? Do you want me to hug you? Do you want me to stay back? Tell me what you want me to do." The fact that her principal connected with her on such a personal level was deeply touching.

Staying Informed and Making Decisions Through Strategic Listening

The principals interviewed directly or indirectly addressed the issue of how they managed to be knowledgeable about what was going on in their respective buildings (Tate, 2002). Most said they visited classrooms and other parts of the school as often as they could, sat in on numerous staff and committee meetings, and deliberately selected department chairs, subject area team leaders, or other key personnel to keep them informed. Even so, they were concerned that there was no way to be aware of everything that affected the success of the school.

In contrast, most of the teachers interviewed were convinced that their principals were very well informed about what went on in the building.

However, the principals and teachers had different perspectives on what it meant to be informed. When the principals discussed how they listened to be informed about the school, they tended to refer mainly to curriculum and personnel issues. Teachers, on the other hand, referred more often to faculty and staff unrest and morale concerns. This was probably due to the different outlooks and responsibilities of the two groups.

All of the principals reported that they used their listening skills to make decisions that affected the school, and they all had some type of formal or informal collaborative decision-making process in place. Once again, they focused on instruction and issues that affected the entire school. For example, several principals described how they sought opinions from teachers regarding the hiring of new staff members. Another described how she asked for and sought faculty input about the design of a new program for the school. The principals seemed comfortable in their sense that their teachers were included in the decision-making process.

All of the teachers interviewed felt that they were included in the decision-making process as well. The kinds of decisions they discussed included the hiring of faculty and staff, the development of school plans, and the design and execution of instruction in their own classrooms. None seemed to doubt whether his or her opinions were important to the principal when it came to making decisions affecting the whole school. In our opinion, this is another example of strategic listening in practice.

One of the most serious frustrations reported by the principals interviewed was the lack of time they had to listen adequately. They knew the value of time spent listening to teachers, but their numerous responsibilities kept them from spending the time necessary to do so. Some principals reported that they worked to increase the time available for teacher communication by arriving at school early, staying late, and taking telephone calls long after students and teachers went home. During the day, they then had more time to roam the halls, hold meetings, observe teachers, and analyze instruction. While they disciplined children, fielded complaints, met with parents, and longed for a few minutes just to stop and think, they listened all the time.

The principals interviewed reported that listening is far more than simply decoding the words that they hear teachers saying: They listen to understand and to make sense of the situation. These principals take many details, such as the background, experiences, or gender of the teachers, into consideration as they work to understand what the spoken words of teachers mean. They observe teachers interacting with colleagues and taking part in meetings. For them, listening is the means to acquire a sense of the contents of teachers' lives and what the words they say mean to them.

The effective principals interviewed use their understanding of their faculties and staffs to build strong relationships and create a positive climate in their building. These principals know what goes on in their buildings pertaining to instruction or morale. They listen to teachers to make wise decisions that benefit the students, staff, and parents. And they reported that their listening to understand paid off in strong instructional programs and a school climate of trust and respect.

A CASE STUDY: STRATEGIC LISTENING ON A SCHOOLWIDE SCALE

Listening strategically to teachers individually and in small groups is hard enough, but listening strategically to a whole room of faculty and staff can be daunting. You can never be sure what teachers are going to say in front of a crowd, and sometimes they're moved to say things you really don't want to hear in front of everyone. However, with planning and patience, listening strategically in large groups can be done successfully. Boone (2001) describes three categories of conversations that you can have in your organization:

- Personal conversations
- Dinner-size conversations
- Mega-conversations

Personal conversations are one-on-one occurrences that can take place in your office or almost anywhere. Dinner-size conversations include three to eight people and are ideal for problem solving and allowing everyone involved to be heard. Individuals can't sit back and hide from the discussion as they can in larger groups (Boone, 2001).

A mega-conversation is used to solve complex problems and create a constructive flow of information. It brings the entire faculty into a shared space and is rich with opportunities to practice strategic listening. What follows are some of the suggestions from Harris (1993) for conducting a successful mega-conversation:

- Decide what you want as a result and be clear on the purpose.
- Make it safe for people to speak up.
- Treat everyone's ideas equally.
- Invite people who have a stake in the issues.
- Break into small discussion groups for at least part of the meeting. Everyone must have an opportunity for input.

- Plan ahead and stay out of the way. Allow groups to solve their own problems.
- Provide structure without being controlling.
- Give time to get results.

These procedures can set the scene for some amazingly productive strategic listening opportunities. What follows is a case study of mega-conversations and strategic listening in a school that needed to change.

STRATEGIC LISTENING AS A TOOL FOR CHANGE

Several years ago, the principal in this case study was appointed to lead a school in a suburban, middle-class neighborhood. Test scores were good, the community was involved, and the few discipline problems that occasionally arose were easily managed. The faculty and community had become comfortable with their success and didn't see the need to instruct or assess students any differently from what they had been doing for years. New teachers fell into the same familiar instructional routines as the rest of the staff. Most students succeeded, but a disquieting number of students did not.

Although teaching strategies had changed little over the years, other changes had occurred in the community and school district. The district placed a program for non-English speakers at the school, because more and more families from countries outside the United States were moving to the area. State-mandated standards were put in place along with sanctions for schools that did not meet them. The No Child Left Behind Act, a federal law that mandated the achievement of all students, was enacted. Because of these factors, it became increasingly clear that the school had to make some major adjustments, and the principal was charged with the responsibility to manage the change process.

Most teachers in this school tended to focus their instruction on students in the middle. Students who needed to accelerate were languishing, and students who struggled were being left behind. Although no one could argue that the teachers were not skilled and compassionate practitioners, it was not uncommon in the building to hear the following reasons for why students did not succeed:

- "He's just lazy. If he tried harder, he'd get better grades."
- "She barely speaks English. There's no way she's going to be successful until she learns the language."
- "If his parents don't care, my hands are tied."

- "The reason the average test scores for my classes are so low is because so many of my students have learning disabilities. Those kids are never going to get it."
- "Everyone knows that the kids on free lunch aren't going to do as well as the others."

To turn this situation around, the faculty and staff needed to take a close look at their personal values and who they were as a school community. They needed to look at best practice, assessment data, and themselves in an open and honest way. This would involve strategic listening on a schoolwide scale.

Getting Started

The school was not the only one in the district that needed to make changes. The district offered staff development training in creating professional learning communities (PLCs) within schools and expected each principal in the district to take advantage of the opportunity.

The fundamental principles of PLCs are simple but powerful. Schools that are PLCs have the following characteristics (DuFour & Eaker, 2000):

- Shared vision, mission, values, and goals
- Collaborative teams focused on learning
- Collective inquiry into best practice and current reality
- Action orientation and experimentation
- Commitment to continuous improvement
- A focus on results

To make the changes at the school in this case study, the initiative had to be guided by teacher leaders who had the respect and trust of the staff. After observing and listening strategically in the school, the principal knew exactly whom she wanted to take the PLC training with her. The teachers she chose were ones who worked hard and had made the effort to incorporate new strategies into their instruction. They were key communicators in the building, and they weren't shy about expressing their thoughts.

Listening Strategically to the Whole Group

Much to their surprise, the teachers selected to lead the process quickly bought into the concept of PLCs and committed themselves to making the concept work at their school. They decided to lead three 2½-hour, site-based, after-school staff development sessions once a month for 3 months. After completing the three staff development sessions, the faculty elected to meet for four more sessions to continue the conversation. The sessions revealed strategic listening on a scale that the principal had never before experienced.

The principal and three lead teachers recognized that there would be serious obstacles to success in this endeavor, and they developed a work session in which teachers were required to share their fears about the process of change. One of the lead teachers spent time discussing the barriers the school would face. He told the faculty, "We have to have the courage to change. In order to be courageous, one must face a frightening situation, person, or idea." He challenged the faculty, as a group, to have the courage to confront each other, their practice, their materials, and themselves. He then asked teachers to write on index cards their fears about the changes involved in becoming a PLC.

After a few minutes, another of the lead teachers collected the cards and read them to the group. As he read off the index cards, the faculty was able to confront its fears and the barriers to its success. The teachers noted that they didn't understand the curricular expectations at different grade levels. They were concerned that, even though they sincerely wanted their students to be successful, they sometimes simply didn't know what to do. Some wrote that they weren't sure that they would be comfortable trusting their coworkers with data that might highlight their weaknesses. Others were concerned about directly confronting colleagues with whom they might have differences.

The principal was gratified to observe that many heads are better than one when it comes to solving problems about students. She saw it as a valuable opportunity for all of the participants to listen strategically and find ways to support their colleagues and assure one another that they were valued.

Listening to Create a Vision

Late one afternoon, the faculty in the case study met in the library to create a new, shared vision statement for the school. The old one had been in existence for a few years and didn't have a lot of meaning for anyone. Basically, it was a pretty-sounding paragraph that was folded into the annual school plan. Now, it was time to forge a vision that meant something.

The principal divided the teachers into six groups, purposely mixing teachers of different grade levels and different specialties to energize the collective thinking. She taped sheets of chart paper to walls in six different parts of the room and instructed the groups to spend 10 minutes at each station responding to the question or statement posted there. When time was up, the groups rotated to the next station. Below are the statements and questions that were posted about the room along with a small sampling of the answers teachers wrote that day.

What makes our school a great place to work?
- Parent and community involvement
- The school has a warm feeling
- Professionalism takes precedence over gossip
- All staff members are supportive
- Students are well behaved
- We have a family atmosphere

I want my school to be a place where . . .
- We can depend on colleagues, parents, and the greater community for support
- Students and staff feel safe, valued, and respected
- There is a diversity of teaching and learning styles
- There is a willingness to try out-of-the-box solutions without fear of failing
- Everyone on the staff looks forward to coming to work

How do we treat each other and our students?
- We are cordial, but isolated sometimes
- At times we avoid dealing with difficult issues directly
- Students are treated fairly
- Sometimes we resort to blaming others out of frustration when we don't know what to do next
- We walk on eggshells with some staff members
- We care about each other

Envision our school five years from now. In what significant ways would you like it to be different than it is today?
- More up-to-date facilities
- More collaboration between teachers and specialists
- Technology would be integrated throughout the curriculum
- A better understanding of curriculum
- More effective use of all resources including personnel

The kind of school I would want my own children to attend would . . .
- Be where they experience success
- Know that they are loved
- Have compassionate, patient teachers

- Be where students learn to love learning
- Feel safe
- Where teachers never give up
- There are high expectations for success

What values would our school embody?
- Good character
- Enthusiasm for learning
- A safe place to take risks
- Where all students succeed
- High efforts by students and teachers are applauded
- No more excuses

The process provided every participant the opportunity to think strategically about what the others were saying and, as a result, practice strategic listening. As teachers took turns reading from the chart paper at the end of the exercise, it was obvious that the school had the beginnings of its vision.

Strategic Listening to Create a School Vision, Mission, and Values

At the next session, one of the lead teachers worked with the teachers to review the information on the charts to find themes and then sort the statements according to the themes. Those themes fell into seven categories that they used to create a new, more meaningful vision statement for the school.

The faculty didn't finish the vision statement during that particular meeting. It took two more after-school meetings to arrive at consensus on what the faculty wanted the school vision to look like. The teachers discussed every syllable of what they thought the school should aspire to be. Although it seemed to be taking a long time, the principal exercised patience, stepped back, and trusted the process. The resulting vision for the case study school is to

- Continuously assess strengths to meet student needs.
- Work collaboratively in teams to regularly and continually monitor student achievement.
- Create and implement learning experiences based on individual needs'
- Strive for a clear and in-depth understanding of ourselves, our students, and each other.

- Embrace technology as a transparent tool for all.
- Promote positive risk-taking for the entire school community.
- Create a safe and comfortable environment.

Next Steps

The school has come a long way from the afternoon the faculty finally agreed on its vision. As a group, the faculty created a mission statement to explain how they would attain the objectives and a set of collective value statements to guide them on the way. The faculty is currently in the process of aligning curriculum across grade levels and planning common assessments.

It wasn't easy. Faculty and staff spent hours agonizing over making decisions about the essential knowledge that they need to teach and assess, and they've been surprised at the perspectives of colleagues they thought they knew well. Nevertheless, they're learning to trust each other more than they've ever done before. Now that the whole faculty and staff are starting to practice listening strategically, the principal expects a big payoff for the students.

RESOURCES

Excerpts From Interviews With Effective
Principals and Selected Faculty Members

The following excerpts are from Tate's (2002) interviews with effective principals and selected faculty members.

Interview Subject 1

Jeanne, a principal for 7 years, told us that she has an open-door policy. When she is in her office, she drops everything she is doing in order to communicate that she is listening to whomever she is with. In spite of her hectic schedule, she tries to give teachers the time they need to talk. She said, "I have to be aware of the listening needs of the person with whom I'm having the conversation and understand where he or she is coming from."

She commented that she thought many of the teachers at her school need a lot of her time and affirmation. In fact, she expressed frustration about the amount of time that teachers seemed to need from her: "I just start to get really irritated with pick, pick, pick, pick, pick, pick, pick. Sometimes during the day, I need a little more of my own space." Then she added, "I just wonder how many years I'm going to be able to keep this up."

Leah was the choral director at Jeanne's school. If Leah noticed that Jeanne occasionally became frustrated with all the demands placed on her, she didn't mention it. Leah described her principal in very warm terms. "She wants to make sure that she listens to everything that everybody says and to every single side of the question. She not only listens, but she asks questions. 'How did the lesson turn out last week?' 'Did you find someone to drive the kids to soccer practice?'" Leah said that if Jeanne was not able to talk to her when she asked, Jeanne set up an appointment for a time when Leah could talk. Even if she were in a hurry to go to a meeting, Jeanne would manage to stop for a couple of minutes. According to Leah, "Jeanne makes time to listen to teachers even when she walks down the hall."

What was significant to Leah was that, when her principal stopped to listen to her, Jeanne seemed to truly care. "When Jeanne talks with teachers in her office, she is all yours. She clears off a special table at the side of the room where she sits with you. So whether you're dropping by or you've made an appointment, she is absolutely committed to you and will stay as long as it takes." Leah added, "Jeanne's number one question is, 'How can I help?'"

Interview Subject 2

Gail, a principal for 12 years, thinks of herself as a good listener. She said that she listens well in meetings and in one-on-one situations. She said, "I always go on little cat feet. I just open my ears . . . and sometimes I won't say anything for a long time. I just listen and listen and listen and listen." By listening, she decides how to deal with an issue. She makes it very clear that she doesn't like to act in an obvious or critical manner if she can do it more discreetly.

When teachers drop by Gail's office, she stops whatever she is doing to listen to them. She said, "Maybe some people would not find that to be the best use of their time. For me, it works, and I wouldn't feel comfortable any other way." She stresses that it's really important for teachers to be able to come and talk to her. She feels that taking the time to listen keeps her aware of what's going on in the building. Even though Gail would prefer to think that she gives everyone the same attention, she said, "Everybody doesn't get the same treatment, because everybody doesn't need the same thing." She admits that she has little patience with chronic complainers. "Listening to the same complaint over and over isn't the best use of my time."

Bob, an English teacher at Gail's school, describes Gail as an intense listener who is open to hearing the viewpoints of different people. He said, "The door to her office is literally always open, and the only time she closes it is when she's in conference or on the phone." He said he knows Gail listens well because she always asks follow-up questions and wants additional information about whatever is discussed. Bob said, "Whatever the circumstances, I always feel as if at that moment, what we were discussing is important and valued."

Interview Subject 3

Frank, another veteran principal, also believes he listens well. He realizes that he needs to get to know his teachers in order to figure out what they really mean when they speak. "A lot of people say one thing and mean something else," he said. "Quite often, there's a message between the lines, and I try to find out what it is." He spends time with teachers in classrooms, in the halls, and wherever else he finds them during the day. He feels that taking the time to ask questions about family members and special interests sends a message to teachers that he cares.

Ed, a special education teacher, describes Frank's leadership style as direct and to the point. He likes the fact that Frank takes notes during many of their conversations, because "that tells me he's paying attention to what I'm saying." Ed describes Frank's open-door policy as "phenomenal." He said, "If he's not tied up in a meeting or on the phone, he will immediately talk about any concern at length. Teachers seem to be Frank's number one priority."

Interview Subject 4

Jim, a principal in a small university community, said that he's been a good listener most of his life. He summed up his style by saying, "I'm comfortable. I listen and I hear." Describing his strategy, he said he looks at teachers' eyes as they speak and he looks "beyond just the words they speak." When he's in his office, he comes out from behind his desk, sits at a table, and makes himself available for as long as teachers want to talk. He can usually tell what kind of mood teachers are in by noticing physical clues. "Teachers might sit forward or slump in their chairs, or they might look at you in the eye or avoid your gaze." He added that blotchy skin is a "dead give away" that a teacher is very concerned about something.

It was interesting that Jim stated that he is a very private person: He said that he never talks with teachers about his family, his vacations, or anything personal unless someone asks him about it. He said he respects the privacy of his teachers and doesn't ask about their personal experiences unless they bring it up first. He never calls teachers in the evening or on weekends, nor does he expect teachers to call him after work. "Personal time outside the building is very important." He said staff members run the gamut from those who never discuss their personal lives to those "who walk in the door and immediately start talking about where they've been, what they've been doing, how they felt about it—the whole thing." The conversations served to give him insight about what is important to the teachers in his building.

Anne, the school librarian, describes Jim's listening style in the following way: "He sits down with me, and gives me his full attention. He doesn't look at anything else while we talk." She also commented on his sense of humor and the respectful way in which he treats students and teachers. "He just enjoys laughing and being able to relate to other human beings."

Anne reported that Jim has an open-door policy. She says that she can schedule time with him if she knows in advance that she needs to talk with him, but "I can always go in any time I want to." She remembered that when she found that she was pregnant with her first daughter, she was nervous about telling him. She had worked for him for only a year and didn't know how he would react to the news. However, she was pleasantly surprised to find that he was excited for her. When she tried to assure him that she would be back the following August, he said, "We'll talk about that later. This is wonderful. Teaching is one part of your life, and we celebrate all parts of your life that you want to share with us." His demonstration of warmth and caring is something that Anne will never forget.

Interview Subject 5

Jack was the most senior principal with whom we spoke. He's been a principal for more than 30 years and is still passionate about school leadership. He said that he learned to listen well through on-the-job experience. "Listening," he said, "is standing back and watching what goes on. You listen with your eyes, and you listen with your ears. Once you get to know people, you can read them. You can read between the lines."

Reading between the lines is important as Jack works with teachers. He said, "Many times people don't know what they want, and they don't know what to do when they get it." Jack said that often what teachers say they want is not the real issue; they just sometimes don't know how to express their concerns in the appropriate words.

Jack explained that he doesn't listen to all teachers with the same intensity. Chronic complainers don't warrant the same attention noncomplainers receive. "There are those people who are always there to complain, and you learn quickly not to pay a whole lot of attention to them. It doesn't matter what you do, because it's never going to be good enough." On the other hand, he makes time immediately for teachers who never complain.

Diana, a science teacher, has worked with Jack for 5 years. She explained that she knows when Jack is really listening by his actions and his body language. "He gives you that eye contact when he's listening to what you are saying." She finds him to be very approachable, and most of the time she doesn't need to make an appointment to see him: "I ask if he has a minute. If he says yes, fine. If not, I go on."

It's Diana's perception that some teachers merit more of Jack's attention than others. "Jack respects certain individuals and what they have to say." Other teachers, whom she referred to as babblers, did not receive much of Jack's time. "I think some of those people get on his last nerve."

Most teachers in the building know when he's approachable. When Jack appears to be preoccupied, she said, "We know not to approach him. We all know what will set him off." Jack has so many issues that arise during the day, Diana says, that he has to prioritize how attentive he can be in his listening. She feels the fact that he is able to focus his listening most of the time, despite being pulled in so many directions, is masterful in itself.

8 Listening to and Presenting Data

A statistician is a person who draws a mathematically precise line from an unwarranted assumption to a foregone conclusion.

—Anonymous

In this chapter, the term *listening* is defined loosely. Naturally, data do not speak; someone has to give the data voice. Few of us are able to comprehend the meaning of numbers that are only spoken, however, so data are commonly presented in three modes: written, graphic, and oral.

You need to listen to all three modes to grasp the full meaning of the data being presented. To look only at charts might cause you to miss meaningful units or intervals. If you read tables with numbers and ignore graphic displays, you may have great difficulty seeing the bigger picture. Yet the worst case might be to look only at written and graphic representations of data and ignore the oral presentation. It is in the latter that the presenter makes his or her interpretation explicit. It is only by listening three ways that you have the potential to gain a clear understanding of

AUTHORS' NOTE: We asked Dr. S. David Brazer, who has special expertise in the unique area of data-driven decision making, to help write this chapter. Dr. Brazer is an Assistant Professor of Education Leadership at George Mason University. Formerly a principal in the Mountain View–Los Altos Union High School District in California, Dr. Brazer came to George Mason University in 1999. He holds a PhD from Stanford University and is an authority in the areas of organization theory, decision making, and site-based management.

data. Remember that the next time you are called upon to present data for one or more key constituencies.

The following scenario introduces our discussion of listening to and presenting data: One of the signature changes our new superintendent implemented in his first year was that each school would make a presentation on student achievement in a school board study session. As principal of one of the two high schools in this very small district, I worked with my assistant principals to look at test scores from the California state assessment program current at the time, grade point averages, Scholastic Aptitude Test (SAT) scores, and college matriculation data. We disaggregated everything by race, gender, free and reduced-price lunch, and grade level. We compiled as slick a PowerPoint presentation as we could, interspersing bar charts with text to demonstrate where we stood with student achievement—the successes and the challenges.

The instructions from the superintendent were not especially specific, because he had never done this with us before. To make sure we were on the right track, he came to school one afternoon with an assistant superintendent to hear and see our presentation. Praising us profusely for being thorough and clear, the superintendent regretfully informed us that we needed to cut our 30-slide presentation down to five, because the board would not have time for such lengthy presentations from each of the district's schools. Panic! How could we say anything meaningful with only five slides?

What our superintendent understood, and what we had yet to learn, was that school boards, other education leaders, and the public in general have a tightly constrained ability to absorb and grasp meaning from data. Yet numbers are powerful. Everyone wants to know the bottom line. Presenting and listening to data are two sides of the coin we think of as communication. If you are able to understand how to *listen* to data, then you will have a better idea about how to *present* it. As a school leader, you are required to do both. Communicating effectively using data means listening to the language of statistics, the language of display, and the language of presentation.

LISTENING TO THE LANGUAGE OF STATISTICS

Numbers strike fear in the hearts of a high proportion of educators. Both master's and doctoral students shake in their boots when first required to study research methods and measures of central tendency (mean, median, and mode); dispersion (standard deviation); and inferential statistics (correlation, regression, chi-square). If you share that fear, then the very next professional development experience you probably should give yourself is a high-quality introductory course on statistics or educational research. In this age of high-stakes testing and results-oriented policies that are strongly biased toward quantifying student achievement, no school leader who wants to avoid numerical analysis can possibly be effective.

There's no space to provide an explanation of statistical methodology in this chapter, but we can provide some illustrations to help you think about how to both listen to and present data in a manner that is statistically valid. We are often sucked into accepting numbers at what appears to be face value and perpetuating common "wisdom" that is simply wrong. It's not that we are incompetent or careless. The problem is that we are not listening to the language of statistics.

Comparing SAT Scores

In our school district in the heart of Silicon Valley in the San Francisco Bay Area, we were in close proximity to three different school districts with excellent high schools and three academically powerful private and parochial high schools. For the portion of the population that could afford to move into wealthy neighborhoods or to pay private school tuition, competition among the high schools was intense. When we entertained high school shoppers, the conversation invariably turned to SAT scores.

Our high school published three years of SAT data in its brochure. We didn't like doing this, because we didn't believe that SAT scores are representative of anything other than individual students' abilities in a narrow band of the curriculum (mathematics and language arts). Furthermore, the College Board, publisher of the SAT, warns against making judgments about school quality on the basis of aggregated SAT scores. When we listened to SAT scores, we heard "individual student aptitude," but parents shopping for a high school heard "school quality."

In an effort to mitigate this problem, we explained to parents that individual SAT data are not intended to be averaged schoolwide, and we cited the College Board as a reputable authority on the subject. If we still had their attention, we further explained that the SAT is designed to yield a nationwide mean of 500 on each test, with a standard deviation of 50. All this means is that approximately 68% of the population taking the SAT will score between 450 and 550, 95% will score between 400 and 600, and 99% will score between 350 and 650. Have your eyes glazed over yet? The real meaning for principals competing for student talent is that comparing schools on the basis of a schoolwide average difference of five points on one test or the other creates a distinction without a meaningful difference and conveys nothing about relative school quality.

Much more meaningful information for parents and others, in our view, was data on college matriculation of the graduating class. Not only were we able to show that approximately 70% of our graduates went directly to 4-year colleges and universities, but we could also point out that 15% to 20% of the class was admitted to the top 25 colleges and universities in the country. We worked hard to get parents to hear that college matriculation data were a much better indicator of school quality than average SAT scores. Without a rudimentary understanding of SAT scores and how they are derived, and without having crunched our numbers on college matriculation, we would have had no hope of doing that.

The Importance of Statistical Error

Whenever political polling is reported on television, the newscaster always reports the margin of error. We know intuitively that if a poll reports that one politician has 47% of the vote and another has 45%, with a margin of error of 3%, the politicians are in a statistical tie. Strangely, statistical error is rarely, if ever, mentioned when examining student test scores.

The No Child Left Behind Act requires all states to set academic standards and test all children in Grades 3–8. States typically set benchmarks that all students must reach in order to be determined academically proficient, competent, basic, or failing. Schools will look at student scores and react accordingly. The problem is that some number of students fail to reach a particular benchmark merely as a random event, because they are inside the margin of error for the test. For such a student, immediate retesting might be a more cost-effective strategy than some more dramatic intervention, such as after-school tutoring.

If principals and teachers are unaware of the margin of error embedded in the tests they give, then they make a less-informed choice about what to do with students who do not meet standards. The typical response is a one-size-fits-all solution (e.g., all classes will spend a certain amount of time reviewing key tested items or all students who "failed" the most recent test are required to attend some sort of remediation). This kind of approach is inefficient and wastes precious instructional time. Worse, our reporting of test scores misrepresents that portion of the student population that is within the margin of error of a particular testing benchmark.

Understanding the scale, the appropriate use of test data, and statistical error are critical to understanding the language of statistics. You can't communicate about these kinds of issues if you don't speak the language. Principals and central office administrators need to know what data tell them in order to be able to listen properly and to convey the data's meaning persuasively to others. Teachers, too, would be well served to understand the language of statistics so that they can communicate effectively with parents about their students' achievement.

LISTENING TO THE LANGUAGE OF DISPLAY

PowerPoint and other presentation programs have put impressive graphics in the hands of all of us. As with any innovation, this is both good and bad. On the good side is that we can produce and edit data displays much more quickly and with better quality than we could 15 years ago. On the negative side, it is now easier than ever to be dazzled by graphics that may be misleading. The classic example of misleading through graphic display is the manipulation of the scale for data. Consider Figures 8.1 and 8.2. They contain real elementary school data from a state testing program.

What do we hear from the different data displays in these figures? If we look quickly at Figure 8.1, it appears that nearly all students are scoring at or above *proficient*. But the maximum of the scale is set at 80%, so without studying the numbers closely, we might be misled to an overly optimistic view of this school's performance. Figure 8.2, in contrast, with the scale maximum set to 100% presents a more realistic picture. Scale is a critical element in the language of display.

Figure 8.1   Third-Grade Reading Scores With the Scale Maximum at 80%

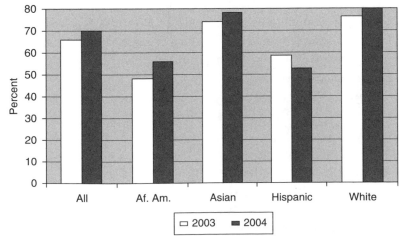

Figure 8.2   Third-Grade Reading Scores With the Scale Maximum at 100%

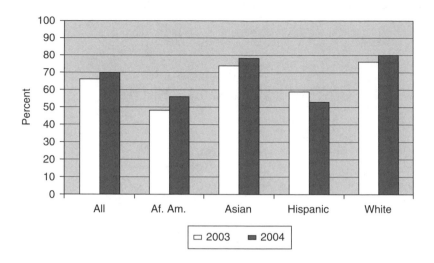

There is still more than meets the eye in both figures. Performance in all categories of students seems to have improved from 2003 to 2004, with the exception of Hispanics. Furthermore, Asians and whites appear to be scoring much higher than African Americans and Hispanics, especially in Figure 8.1—the classic achievement gap problem. But only percentages are reported. This particular school has just over 100 students in the third grade, making the numbers of students in any given ethnic category relatively small. Percentages can be misleading with small numbers.

We manipulated the data in Figure 8.3 just a bit to demonstrate the volatility of percentages when small numbers are involved. For 2004, we increased the number of African American and Hispanic students who scored *proficient* and above by three each. We also reduced the number of Asians and whites who scored *proficient* and above by three each. By changing the results of only 12 students in the third grade, the achievement gap nearly disappears.

The point in this exercise is that displaying only percentages can be quite deceptive. Consumers of statistical information need to know the absolute size of the group in question—their *n* in statistical parlance. The small changes we made in the 2004 data suggest that the achievement gap problem at this particular elementary school is not as great as it first appeared in Figures 8.1 or 8.2. This is not to suggest that the school should work less on improving student achievement, but it does help to put the problem into perspective. Instead of focusing on an achievement gap that

Figure 8.3   Third-Grade Reading Scores—Increasing African Americans and Hispanics by Three Students and Decreasing Asians and Whites by Three Students

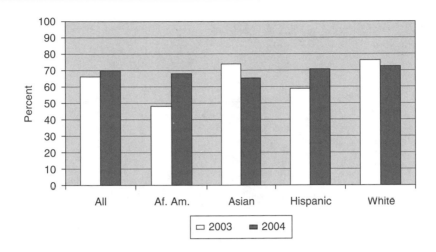

is, in reality, small or nonexistent, this particular school probably ought to be concentrating on helping all students to achieve at a higher level.

PowerPoint, and other programs like it, is a valuable tool in the language of display. Unfortunately, it is often misused. Display programs should be seen as aides to oral presentations, not stand-alone documents. Too often, presenters put their whole presentation into their slides, and then proceed to read the slides to the audience. This has the negative effect of both insulting listeners and putting them to sleep. Most presentation experts recommend that verbiage in slides be kept to a minimum and used only as cues to the presenter and the listeners. Figure 8.4 is an illustration of how we might use the data manipulation from Figure 8.3 in a slide presentation.

The sample PowerPoint slide (see Figure 8.4) combines graphics and few words to convey basic meaning to the listening audience. The title questions the existence of an achievement gap at this elementary school, and the bulleted statements convey the speaker's interpretation of the data. All that is left for the speaker to do is to flesh out the explanation in the oral presentation.

Data displays emanate from a particular interpretation of data and should be viewed with caution. Effective displays enhance, but are not designed to replace, a verbal explanation of what the data mean. You should avoid looking only at displays divorced from their explanations, because your interpretation may not be the same as that of the display's creator. Likewise, when presenting your own displays, never assume that they

Figure 8.4   Sample PowerPoint Slide

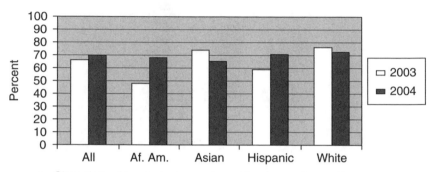

- Changing a few students creates a big change in results
- Focus on boosting all, rather than differences between groups

speak for themselves, because they can't. A presentation that contains your interpretation is vital to your persuasiveness about what the data mean.

LISTENING TO THE LANGUAGE OF PRESENTATION

As school leaders, we are often required to attend school board meetings, and many of us may use them as a relatively quiet place to read mail that has piled up. However, we should put aside our mail when a school official presents something as important to us as budget or student achievement data, because this information is central to the operation of an effective school. If the presentation isn't engaging, we might find our mail more interesting and miss important cues about where the district administration and the school board are headed.

You may, because of fear, a basic lack of interest, or poor skills on the part of the presenter, find data presentations boring. However, you need to overcome any tendencies you may have to be bored by such presentations. Data are often politically charged, and the presenter's interpretation of that data via oral presentation is important information regarding the position the district is taking on it. For example, is this year's budget deficit seen as a one-time aberration or a dangerous harbinger of the district's fiscal future? Is your school's achievement data interpreted as a red flag, normal results, or an exemplar for the district? Answers to these questions are embedded in the data presentation and provide important perspectives to you as an education leader. They indicate to you whether you need to make changes, celebrate success, or fight back with alternative interpretations of your own.

To be an effective school leader who understands and manages the communication about your school or district requires an ability to understand the language of presentation, which is in turn based on an understanding of the languages of statistics and statistical displays. You need to determine if the presentation being made is faithful to the data and the displays in the presentation. If your interpretation and that of the presenter are consistent, then you know you agree on the available facts. If they are inconsistent, then you may have a problem. You need to check your own understanding first, and if it is valid, then you need to start asking yourself why the presenter wants to promote an alternative interpretation. What you hear through presentations and the presentations' consistency with the data as you understand it gives you important information about the priorities and perspectives of the presenter. It is then up to you as a leader to decide what to do about it.

Just as with the language of statistics and the language of display, you are both a receiver and a transmitter of the language of presentation. Some authors claim that most people fear public speaking more than death. This may be a myth, but we feel confident saying that most people dread listening to presentations of data. It is your job as presenter to help your audience overcome the desire to run screaming from the room by engaging them in what you have to say. Humor helps, but not everyone is a stand-up comedian. Presentations often fail to reach their audiences because their main point is unclear or not demonstrated: They are not well organized, they are not well supported visually, they are too long, or they are a combination of all of these factors. Common folks like us can make presentations work if we follow some basic guidelines.

Your presentation should start with a thesis, the point you will prove through the course of the presentation. This is always true, but particularly with presentations of data. The audience should know within the first minute of your talk what you intend for them to understand by the time you are finished. Without this, they will quickly get lost and you will have a greater tendency to ramble.

Use the thesis of your presentation to organize it. The order of ideas in the thesis should be the same as the order of your detailed explanations. By maintaining this kind of parallel construction, you make it much easier for your listeners to follow your logic. If they do that, you have a higher probability of persuading them that your interpretation is correct.

Use the kinds of visual cues discussed above in the Listening to the Language of Display section. If you use slides, make them clear and vivid, and avoid putting too much text into them. Refer to your slides frequently to support what you are saying so that you communicate in at least two modes—but never read them. Your visual aides and your speech should complement one another, and each should be a necessary ingredient of your presentation.

The best conceived presentations fail when they go on past the listener's ability to concentrate on one subject or when they provide information the listener doesn't need or doesn't care about. It is often difficult to gauge listener receptivity to a specific topic. You can cope with this uncertainty by keeping your one-way communication brief and allowing ample time for a question-and-answer session as part of your presentation. We suggest that you discipline yourself to speak no longer than 15 minutes before asking for questions, comments, and clarifications. Your listeners will be grateful, which may predispose them to agree with you.

The language of presentation is all about interpretation and persuasion. Be a skeptical consumer of presentations by using your knowledge of statistics and your understanding of displays to check for consistency. Similarly, be consistent in your own presentations as you work to persuade your listeners about the meaning of the data you present.

LISTENING TO AND LEADING WITH DATA

The rapidly proliferating clichés around accountability, high-stakes testing, and data-driven decision making suggest that you, as a member of this generation of education leaders, will be coping with data in many different ways if you want to survive and excel in your schools and districts. If you embrace this reality and develop your skills with data just as you have with other aspects of your job responsibilities, you will have little to fear in a realm that terrifies many educators. More important, when you become the kind of leader who can listen to and convey the meaning of data in ways that help you and others to understand educational realities, you will serve your students and your school communities far more effectively.

9 Considerations for Your Own Practice

I listen fine. It's the others who have a problem.

—Anonymous

Strategic listening is a complex activity, and its complexity explains the emphasis given in previous chapters to understanding the processes and types of listening. We spend an inordinate amount of our time in conversation. We know that one of the many measures of our effectiveness on the job is that our constituencies seldom feel or complain about being ignored or neglected. And even though one of the hardest things to do in life is to listen without intent to reply, we listen patiently to everyone, acknowledge what they have to say, and demonstrate that we understand.

Sometimes, our listening agenda is enough to send us home dog-tired at the end of the day. Sometimes, we just feel like we'd like to dump strategic listening, and when Joe or Sally or Fred or Mary is talking to us, we'd like to interrupt him or her and say something like, "You know, I'm glad I'm smarter than you," or, "You think you've got it tough?" Sometimes, we'd like to pepper the conversation with statements like, "You know, Joe, you're really boring me; that's crazy, stupid, immature." At other times, we may want to let our minds wander: ". . . Mary, I'm sorry, I was thinking about the great gourmet dinner I had last night. . . . Was there a point you were trying to make?"

Or maybe we'd prefer to practice nothing but strategic *thinking* while others are talking. It would be so relaxing to drop the listening skills that have made us effective in the eyes of our followers and just adopt a listening stance that allows us to read the mind of the speaker, daydream often, or remember and savor personal experiences instead of listening.

Another appealing, but dangerous, strategy would be to consider every conversation an intellectual debate with the goal of putting down our opponent. It could be fun just to wait for the moment when we can laugh off what the speaker is saying and quickly change the topic or just placate him or her by saying, "You're right . . . of course . . . I agree!" And finally, when someone directs unpleasant or hostile emotions at us, it would be great to shout, "Buzz off!" "Get a life!"—or something worse.

It's not easy to actively listen and demonstrate empathy all the time. Strategic listening is clearly a complex skill and can be exhausting, but it's an important part of our job as effective leaders. Strategic listening shows that we care and that we understand the speaker. It allows speakers to accept us as listeners and invites them to tell their story and express, sometimes vent, their feelings. It fosters more meaningful, helpful interactions and strengthens others' aggregate impression of us as effective leaders.

THE ESSENCE OF STRATEGIC LISTENING

Consider strategic listening as part of your thinking process, the cognitive domain of learning. Strategic listening doesn't just happen; it takes thought. Make sure that you do the following:

• *Prepare to listen.* Listening, simply defined, is the act of opening your ears and mind when a speaker opens his or her mouth. When confronted with a situation in which the speaker's emotions are centered on your actions or inactions, you need to practice extreme willpower. Inevitably, speakers, when emotionally charged, make some remarks that you probably feel you must put to rest immediately. The trouble is, if you do this, it sends the whole exchange off on tangential arguments, and the speaker gets more frustrated in not being able to reach the important point. Remember remarks to be countered later; let the speaker finish. You will benefit from the fact that the speaker's anger has diminished markedly.

• *Adjust to the situation.* No listening situation is exactly the same as another. The time, the environment, the speaker, and the message all change. Effective leaders, as is true of effective theatrical actors, know that their first responsibility, when on stage, is to find the light, play the reality, and be aware of the audience.

• *Let a bit of intuition into your listening process.* Don't prejudge what a speaker has to say, but don't forget that you didn't get where you are today without a wealth of experiences behind you. Don't hesitate to make use of your life experiences or gut reactions, when you're helping someone resolve a problem or listening to make a decision. Intuition, sometimes labeled "smart guessing," will more often than not lead you down the right path in attempting to help someone in need. The same is true with decision making.

If we have learned anything in working in our nonlinear world of education, it's simply that there is no substitute for *paying attention.* Every school is alive with distinct, stimulating, and often unpredictable events each day. The school environment comprises a web of interrelationships between human beings who have much in common, but are often in conflict and require our constant attention. We've learned that a major part of being attentive is listening, and that our listening skills are as powerful a means of communication and influence as the way we present ourselves through speech and behavior. Furthermore, successful education leadership involves the difficult task of bringing diverse people together to accomplish specific goals, and much of this leading is about recognizing and appreciating different perspectives.

Success as a school leader depends on one's ability to work effectively with competing interests and multiple constituencies. Effective school leaders we've observed have developed both tolerance for ambiguity and refined listening skills, and they balance their allegiances and loyalties in ways that ensure that no individual or group feels unimportant, not listened to, or left out.

In our experience, when working with multiple constituencies, language, as a medium, is most effective when used to create meaning and shared understanding rather than simply to exchange information. Conversations reflect two or more sets of experiences, ours and another person's, and strategic listeners offer everyone the opportunity to contribute to the development of shared meaning. Because we all filter conversations through our own unique set of beliefs and experiences, effective leaders work to see the world through the eyes of their constituents and acknowledge the value of their unique perspectives. When leaders enable the participants in a conversation to listen as a group for collective meaning, a whole new world of possibilities opens, enabling them to listen to, engage with, and integrate special interests and multiple constituencies and blend them effectively into a working unit.

School leaders who practice strategic listening understand that it is not just the speaker's responsibility to make sure that he or she is understood, but also that the listener has a major role to play in hearing the complete message. In face-to-face interactions, not every piece of information is presented at all times, so strategic listeners continuously interpret what they hear. They use their listening skills to increase their opportunities to get the most complete and accurate message possible so they can respond constructively.

The essence of strategic listening can be summarized in seven basic concepts.

1. Strategic listeners give 100% of their attention to the speaker. They limit the amount of talking they do, because you can't really listen when you're talking. They look and act interested to show that they care about what the speaker is saying. They suspend other activities for the moment and try to put the speaker at ease so that he or she feels free to talk. In addition, they listen intuitively. That is, they review and consider past experiences, previous encounters, and prior conversations that are related to or have an impact on the current interaction. And they avoid judging from their own perspective, using the skill of decentering to differentiate their point of view from that of the speaker.

To enhance your strategic listening skills, consider the following in your own practice:

- Focus on the speaker and avoid interrupting as much as possible.
- Create a receptive environment.
- Demonstrate respect for the worth of the speaker and his or her position and perspective.
- Ignore preconceptions you may have.
- Listen with sensitivity.
- Address and diminish any threat that might exist in the mind of the speaker.
- Recognize and use behaviors that let speakers know you are listening.
- Use open-ended questions to prompt speakers for in-depth information. Your objective is to get them to talk freely and as much as possible.

2. Strategic listeners use both verbal and nonverbal responses. They seek to demonstrate to the speaker that they received and understood the message, and more important, they show that it had an impact on their thinking. They recognize that just saying something like, "I understand," is not enough. They confirm their understanding and the impact of the message by occasionally restating the main ideas in the message to let the

speaker know that they get it. They don't just repeat the words they heard, but restate them to prove they understand. These two methods transmit dramatically different messages to the speaker and can have a major impact on the results. Strategic listeners also consciously avoid the use of "tune out" or "turn off" words in any prompts they give.

To enhance your strategic listening skills, consider the following in your own practice:

- Acknowledge the information—both verbal and nonverbal—that others convey to you.
- Use feedback to clarify and confirm your understanding and minimize the use of direct, closed-ended questions that can put the speaker on the defensive.
- Structure your feedback for positive results. Provide feedback based on your best understanding of the speaker's ideas, views, and needs.
- Be patient and give the speaker time to communicate.
- Lubricate conversations with compliments and positive reinforcement.

3. Strategic listeners pay attention to nonverbal signs of the speaker's inner feelings, such as voice quality, facial expressions, body posture, and motions. Nonverbal cues are revealing and sometimes contradict the speaker's words. Strategic listeners concentrate on identifying hidden emotional meanings. They ask themselves, *What are the real feelings behind the speaker's words? What does the tone of voice connote? What does the emphasis on certain words mean?* And they understand that what people hesitate to say is often the most critical element. When strategic listeners are successful at decoding the meaning of nonverbal behavior, those with whom they interact perceive them more positively.

To enhance your strategic listening skills, consider the following in your own practice:

- Observe and evaluate nonverbal cues and the speaker's emotional state.
- Use your emotions effectively and leave your personal baggage at home.
- Listen to discover the speaker's hidden assumptions.
- Avoid mistaking inferences for facts.
- Read between the lines.
- Incorporate your observations into your thinking process.

4. Strategic listeners consider other people's views, concerns, or questions seriously. They avoid using patronizing statements like, "I appreciate your position" or "I know how you feel." Such statements are often

followed by a phrase beginning with the word "but" that negates their meaning. In addition, strategic listeners match their communication to the others' levels of understanding and feeling. They attempt to do this as naturally as possible and use their tone of voice, rate of speech, and choice of words to show that they are trying to completely understand the speaker's situation at that moment. When you accurately read another person's point of view, it is much easier to work with that person from his or her perspective. Strategic listeners know that connecting with speakers in a precise and believable way promotes positive communication.

They also recognize that when emotions are high, there is a tendency to tune out the speaker, become defensive, or want to give premature advice, so they control their tempers (no matter how difficult it may be) to keep their own emotions from interfering with their listening. They know you don't have to agree to be a good listener if you listen to understand, not confront.

To enhance your strategic listening skills, consider the following in your own practice:

- Don't preach, moralize, or patronize.
- Recognize your own personal biases that block strategic listening.
- Put yourself in the speaker's moment.
- Suspend judgment and maintain a neutral observer mode; be curious, not aggressive.
- Identify and prioritize the essential factors before responding.
- Express your opinions while still acknowledging the other person's opinions as valid.
- Focus on areas of agreement rather than differences.
- Aim for a mutually satisfactory solution.

5. Strategic listeners recognize that there are cultural barriers to strategic listening that can lead to misunderstanding. Cultural differences can be based on gender, ethnicity, nationality or regionality, religion, and even age and lifestyle. The meaning of words can change from situation to situation and from one culture or subculture to another, so strategic listeners define meaning as unique and appropriate to the current situation and to the people immediately involved. They are aware that the culture in which we grow up greatly influences how we interpret the messages we receive from others. When individuals from two different cultures speak, there may be two different behavioral norms in evidence, and it's very likely that there may be two very different worldviews selectively screening information. What is considered effective communication in one culture or subculture can be misunderstood or considered inappropriate in another culture or subculture.

To enhance your strategic listening skills, consider the following in your own practice:

- Pay attention to and respect cultural or subcultural differences.
- Listen to understand the culture the speaker represents.
- Make appropriate adjustments in your listening and responses using appropriate, culturally correct eye contact and expressions to encourage dialogue.

6. The best overall strategic listeners we have observed continually read their audiences and use that ability to develop a constituent following. Simply stated, strategic listeners listen up front. They diagnose people's inclinations and the logical content of their thoughts, needs, and wants. They work to understand precisely what it will take to provide leadership, contribute to teamwork, offer assistance, solve problems, or advance opportunities. Then, they act decisively on what they've heard and learned. They are continuously aware of the perception development process through which they can consciously reinforce their aggregate impression as a leader in the eyes of their constituents.

To enhance your strategic listening skills, consider the following in your own practice:

- Accept the ambiguity inherent in your environment.
- Be proactive in addressing your multiple constituencies.
- Seek the bottom line to problem resolution.
- Actively work to influence other people's perceptions of you and identify which of your behaviors strengthen or weaken other people's aggregate impression of you.

7. Strategic listeners consider communication a *people process* rather than a *language process*, and they see strategic listening as a strategy that enables them to effectively receive and transmit both oral and written messages.

To enhance your strategic listening skills, consider the following in your own practice:

- Recognize how cognition, language, and behavior interrelate and affect communication.
- Recognize that strategic listening is not a solo performance; it's a connection, and it's most successful when circular.

Listening to and acknowledging speakers may seem to be deceptively simple, but doing it well, particularly when disagreements arise, takes talent and skill. And, as is true with any skill, strategic listening takes practice. We continuously practice our strategic listening skills and aim for the kind of verbal and nonverbal responses that validate the success of our efforts. Our goal is to get responses from speakers that tell us they felt that we listened as if we honestly wanted to hear what they had to say, and that we gave their words appropriate and respectful consideration.

References

Bennis, W. (1997). *Managing people is like herding cats.* Provo, UT: Executive Excellence.

Bogotch, I. E., & Roy, C. P. (1997). The contexts of partial truths: An analysis of principals' discourse. *Journal of Educational Administration, 35,* 234–252.

Boone, M. E. (2001). *Managing interactively: Executing business strategy, improving communication, and creating a knowledge-sharing culture.* New York: McGraw-Hill.

Borisoff, D., & Hahn, D. F. (1997). Listening and gender: Values revalued. In M. Purdy & D. Borisoff (Eds.), *Listening in everyday life: A personal and professional approach* (pp. 55–75). Lanham, MD: University Press of America.

Brownell, J. (1993). Listening environment: A perspective. In A. D. Wolvin & C. G. Coakley (Eds.), *Perspectives on listening* (pp. 3–27). Norwood, NJ: Ablex.

Donaldson, G. A. (1991). *Learning to lead: The dynamics of the high school principalship.* Westport, CT: Greenwood.

DuFour, R., & Eaker, R. (2000). *Professional learning communities at work: Practices for enhancing student achievement.* Bloomington, IN: National Educational Service.

Dunklee, D. R. (1999). *You sound taller on the telephone.* Thousand Oaks, CA: Corwin.

Dunklee, D. R. (2000). *If you want to lead, not just manage: A primer for principals.* Thousand Oaks, CA: Corwin.

Dyer, K. M., & Corothers, J. (2000). *The intuitive principal: A guide to leadership.* Thousand Oaks, CA: Corwin.

Ellinor, L., & Gerard, G. (1998). *Dialogue: Rediscover the transforming power of conversation.* New York: Wiley.

Freud, S. (1927). *The ego and the id.* London: Hogarth.

Gleick, J. (1988). *Chaos: Making a new science.* New York: Viking.

Gronn, P. (1983). Talk as work: The accomplishments of school administration. *Administrative Science Quarterly, 28,* 1–21.

Harris, T. E. (1993). *Applied organizational communication: Perspectives, principals, and pragmatics.* Hillsdale, NJ: Lawrence Erlbaum.

Helgesen, S. (1990). *The female advantage: Women's ways of leadership.* New York: Doubleday.

Helgesen, S. (1995). *The web of inclusion.* New York: Doubleday.

Johnson, J. (1993). Functions and process of inner speech in listening. In A. D. Wolvin & C. G. Coakley (Eds.), *Perspectives in listening* (pp. 29–53). Norwood, NJ: Ablex.

Knapp, M. L., & Hall, J. A. (2002). *Nonverbal communication in human interaction.* Belmont, CA: Wadsworth.

Lederer, F. L. (2000). Hearing. *Encarta Encyclopedia.* Redmond, WA: Microsoft.

Marlow, M. (1992). Inspiring trust. *Executive Excellence, 9*(12), 12–15.

Morris, R. L., Crowson, R., Porter-Gehrie, C., & Hurwitz, E. (1984). *Principals in action.* Columbus, OH: Merrill.

Peters, T., & Austin, N. (1985). *A passion for excellence: The leadership difference.* New York: Random House.

Purdy, M. (1997). What is listening? In M. Purdy & D. Borisoff (Eds.), *Listening in everyday life: A personal and professional approach* (pp. 1–16). Lanham, MD: University Press of America.

Rothlesberger, F. J. (1995). Of words and men. In S. T. Corman, S. P. Banks, C. R. Bantz, & M. E. Meyer (Eds.), *Foundations of organizational communication* (pp. 88–96). White Plains, NY: Longman.

Schrange, M. (1989). *No more teams! Mastering the dynamics of creative collaboration.* New York: Doubleday.

Schulte, B. (2004, July 26). Teaching teachers how to connect with urban students. *Washington Post,* p. B1.

Shockley-Zalabak, P. (2002). *Fundamentals of organizational communication: Knowledge, sensitivity, skills, values.* Boston: Allyn & Bacon.

Shotter, J. (1993). *Conversational realities: Constructing life through language.* Thousand Oaks, CA: Sage.

Tannen, D. (1990). *You just don't understand: Men and women in conversation.* New York: William Morrow.

Tannen, D. (1998). *The argument culture.* New York: Random House.

Tate, J. (2002). *Sense-making strategies of school leaders: The specific impact of listening.* Unpublished doctoral dissertation, George Mason University, Fairfax, VA.

Thomlinson, T. D. (1997). Intercultural listening. In M. Purdy & D. Borisoff (Eds.), *Listening in everyday life: A personal and professional approach* (pp. 79–120). Lanham, MD: University Press of America.

Twain, M. (1882). "On the decay of the art of lying." *Great Literature Online.* Retrieved December 3, 2004, from www.underthesun.cc/Classics/Twain/artoflying/

Waller, W. (1965). *The sociology of teaching.* New York: Wiley.

Walsh, P. (1998, December 6). A for effort, but F for too much. *Washington Post,* p. C5.

Wolvin, A., & Coakley, C. G. (1996). *Listening.* New York: McGraw-Hill.

Index

**CORWIN
PRESS**

The Corwin Press logo—a raven striding across an open book—represents the union of courage and learning. Corwin Press is committed to improving education for all learners by publishing books and other professional development resources for those serving the field of K–12 education. By providing practical, hands-on materials, Corwin Press continues to carry out the promise of its motto: **"Helping Educators Do Their Work Better."**